COFFEE TALK

COFFEE TALK

Navigating Through Christian Womanhood

MICHELLE HICKS

TATE PUBLISHING
AND ENTERPRISES, LLC

Coffee Talk
Copyright © 2014 by Michelle Hicks. All rights reserved.

No part of this publication may be reproduced, stored in a retrieval system or transmitted in any way by any means, electronic, mechanical, photocopy, recording or otherwise without the prior permission of the author except as provided by USA copyright law.

Scripture quotations marked "NIV" are taken from the *Holy Bible, New International Version* ®, Copyright © 1973, 1978, 1984 by International Bible Society. Used by permission of Zondervan Publishing House. All rights reserved.

The opinions expressed by the author are not necessarily those of Tate Publishing, LLC.

Published by Tate Publishing & Enterprises, LLC
127 E. Trade Center Terrace | Mustang, Oklahoma 73064 USA
1.888.361.9473 | www.tatepublishing.com

Tate Publishing is committed to excellence in the publishing industry. The company reflects the philosophy established by the founders, based on Psalm 68:11,
"The Lord gave the word and great was the company of those who published it."

Book design copyright © 2014 by Tate Publishing, LLC. All rights reserved.
Cover design by Rachel Hicks and Allen Jomoc
Interior design by Rachel Hicks and Jake Muelle

Published in the United States of America

ISBN: 978-1-63268-151-5
Religion / Christian Life / Women's issues
14.07.15

DEDICATION

This book is dedicated to the Lord Jesus, who taught me the life lessons that are in this book and whose idea this book was to begin with. God initially created my personality to be shy and overly sensitive, but He has grown me out of that shyness and sensitivity each year that I age so that I can become a more obedient vessel for Him to use for His purposes.

In October, 2008, Gary and I were attending a pastor's conference in Amarillo, TX, and while we were there the following words were prophesied over me:

"Michelle, I believe that the Lord is saying that He is really going to use you in a mighty way. You will be ministering to women and praying over them. I see a real destiny for you. The Lord is calling that forth in you and He is going to raise you up and He is going to purpose you. He is going to give you a new vision, a new understanding, and is going to "define" the places in you that He is going to cultivate. I believe the Lord would continue to say that you have 'words of power' and 'words of life.' As you teach other women to confess these words over their lives, their husbands, and their families then He will get the glory. You are supposed to teach it and then to "walk it out." There is a fulfilling, almost like an "inner spring; rivers of living water" that will flow out of you as you just begin to speak over women how to bless their family with their words. And you are going to write teachings based upon what you have learned about how to confess and bless your family and

how to create that home and that spiritual atmosphere in the home."

My initial reaction was shock, awe, and the shy girl saying: "Yah, right!" But within a month of being home, this book poured out from inside me into the laptop. Glory to God that this is all His doing in my life!

All I am is a conduit for God to use for His glory!

At the next pastor's conference in October, 2009, the following was prophesied over me: *"The book of Isaiah says that: "The Spirit of the Sovereign Lord is upon you." Michelle, He has anointed you! He has anointed you to preach the good news to the broken-hearted! I believe that He is going to be opening doors for you with broken women…to really encourage them. You have a story to tell and you have paid the cost to share your story. God is putting you in the pulpit to preach to other women because He has given you a strong message to share." "I also saw a vision of you as you were standing up preaching that your tongue was like a sword. And as I saw you speaking with the authority of God I saw shackles falling off of women who were in serious bondage. I also heard the Lord say that it is time to be transparent because your transparency is really going to touch the women in a great way."*

I choose to share this with you to make sure you understand that what pours out of my heart through out these pages is to use the gift of encouragement that God has given me to help other women as you walk your individual walk in life. Life is hard! But God is good and faithful!

I also want to thank God for my family who are His precious gifts to me. Thank you, Gary, for helping me to become the woman I am today. You allowed me to blossom into the flower God had destined for me to become through unconditional love, support, and encouragement. I love you and thank God for blessing me with you.

I am so blessed and honored to have our four children, Rebekah, Joshua, Rachel, and James. Each one of you is a special and precious gift from God to me and I am so proud of each one of you individually.

Rebekah Michelle: You have blossomed into an incredible woman of God and I am honored to be your mom. Thanks for being such a wonderful first-born guinea pig and not allowing our mistakes as we grew in parenting to keep you from becoming all God has planned for you to be. I am so proud of your love for God, others, and your desire to serve Him as a worship leader/song writer. I look forward to seeing all God does through your worship album. Look for Rebekah Michelle music at: iTunes or Amazon.

Joshua David: What a man of God you have become! You have been such a blessing to our family and stepped up as my strong leader while your father has been sick. Thank you for applying all the wonderful traits Gary taught you as you were growing up. I am so proud of the man of God, lawn/lot business man and bass player you have become. I look forward to seeing all God plans to do with and in your life as you continue to serve Him wholeheartedly.

Rachel Meagan: I am still in awe of the talents God has blessed you with at such a young age. You are an incredible photographer and being self-taught just astounds me. All I did was birth in you the love of pictures and God in you did the rest. The fact that you are already photographing weddings before you are 18 years old is a testament to the faithfulness of God in your precious life. I am so proud of how you love God, your family and others and want to serve Him with all your heart. I rejoice with you as you continue to become all He has destined for you to be.

James Daniel: You are as tall as Joshua already and still growing. I am so proud of the godly man you are becoming. I love how you have learned and worked under all of our family businesses to become the well-rounded fifteen year old that you are. From daycare to lawn service to photography or playing bass guitar, wherever you are needed you are willing to serve and do it well. I look forward to seeing all that God plans to do in and through your life as your father's twin, 33 years apart. ;-)

Thank you also to my parents, Don and Jan Hill, who offered me a Godly, Christian-ministry home to grow up in. They gave me a secure, loving and God-centered foundation to build my life upon.

And thank you to my sisters, Maranatha and Elizabeth, and to Gary's parents, Ted and Zell Hicks, who have always been loving and supportive of me. I love you all so much!

ACKNOWLEDGEMENTS

Grateful acknowledgment is made to the following for permission to reprint copyrighted material:

Taken from My Utmost for His Highest by Oswald Chambers, © 1935 by Dodd Mead & Co., renewed © 1963 by Oswald Chambers Publications Assn., Ltd. Used by permission of Discovery House Publishers, Grand Rapids MI 49501. All rights reserved.

Excerpted from: How to Forgive When You Don't Feel Like It
Copyright © 2007 by Hope for the Heart, Inc.
Published by Harvest House Publishers, Eugene, OR
Used by Permission. www.harvesthousepublishers.com

Conclusion: taken from GotQuestions.org. Used by permission.
Excerpts from *Streams in the Desert* and *Springs in the Valley* by Mrs. Charles E. Cowman.

CONTENTS

Introduction 13
Daily Time With Jesus 17
God's Will for My Life. 33
Learn Yourself. 43
Make Yourself a Priority Too! 47
We're in a War! 51
Love Without Reserve 57
Much Grace and Forgiveness 63
We're All Unique! So Don't Judge! 69
We are All Gifted! 75
Contentment & Thankfulness 79
Be a Good Listener! Tame Your Tongue! 83
Attitude 89
Respect and Honor. 93
Communication in Marriage 99
Be an Encourager! 105
God Will Provide! 109
Opposite Sex Guidelines and Intimacy with
    Your Husband 113
Children are a Blessing! Parenting is a Marathon,
    Not a Sprint! 121
We All Have the Same Kids! 127

Home-Schooling Verses Public or Private
    Schooling. 131
God Works All Things Together for Good! 137
When Our Fear Collides with Our Faith! 141
Adversity: God's Tool to Mature Us 147
God (*Disciples*) Disciplines Those He Loves! 155
God's "Waiting Room" 161
Don't Give Up! Life is Hard…But God is Good! . . . 167
Take Me! Bless Me! Crush Me! Use Me! 173
God Knows and Walks with Each of Us
    Individually! 179
Eternity Drives Me Forward 183
Focus on Today! 189
The Law of Opposition: Grow or Die 193
Sickness 199
Conclusion: The Plan of Salvation;
    Rededication to God 207

INTRODUCTION

The path of a woman is full of many changes and challenges. The rules and boundaries of our lives fluctuate based on each season of life we are in. Being a woman is very difficult at times, but very rewarding. Only we can be pregnant and birth God's blessing of children. God has uniquely made us to be His nurturers of people. He has designed us to keep our society and culture from becoming distant and uncaring of human touch and love. We do this by exhibiting the desire to be kind and generous to everyone we come in contact with. Through our nurturing love we offer consistent touch, encouraging words, home-cooked meals, and a home environment that is full of love as well as a safe haven from the outside world. All of these hidden labors are what keep our society from self-destructing.

My desire is to encourage each woman with some nuggets of truth that I have gleaned along my path of womanhood. These truths have helped me navigate and survive the many seasons of my life. All of these principles are to encourage you as you walk *"your road of womanhood."* Don't use any of these thoughts to bring condemnation on yourself. Instead, pray about each one. If it is confirmed in your spirit that God would have you apply this to your life, then ask Him for His help to begin the changes. As a pastor's wife I love talking to and sharing with other women "one-on-one." This book contains some of the things I would share with each woman if we sat down with some coffee to discuss any of the following topics.

I want to clarify that I have had the privilege of being a stay-at-home mom for nineteen years and have tons of respect for all of the working outside-of-the-home moms of today. You are working two full-time jobs. To you, I especially ask that you not take on any condemnation from anything you read in this book. You are juggling an incredible load and are not expected to be a perfect *superwoman*. Recently I have worked for 1 ½ years outside the home at an in-home daycare averaging 33 hours a week. Then the Lord led me to open my own in-home daycare caring for 12 children and my hours have now jumped to 60+ hours a week. The blessing is I am back at home which is where I love to be. Be encouraged that no matter what your daily life responsibilities are…God desires to be involved at every juncture!

An important understanding that God has taught me is that He cares as much about the "process" of growing closer to Him as He does about the "end result." If we think it through, we will realize that we never arrive at spiritual maturity anyway. God is too infinite for us to fathom and our minds are too finite for us to learn all there is to know about Him. We won't fully be mature in Christ until we are in heaven with Him. This doesn't mean that we stop putting effort into growing spiritually mature. It just takes the pressure off of us by thinking we will attain perfection on this earth.

God is crazy about you! He is massively in love with you and He enjoys every step of the process of revealing

Himself to you personally and helping you to grow in your relationship with Him. He desires to heal you and set you free from all your past hurts through the truths in His Word. In this book we will discuss many of the Scriptural principles that He wants us to apply to our lives. We will discuss many of the areas that God challenges each one of us to grow in as we mature in Christ. You will never get bored with God because there is always more to learn.

This book can be read in its entirety or you can read a chapter a day for a whole month and have more time to learn from and apply whatever the Spirit of God encourages you to take from it.

To each woman of God I challenge you to glean what you can and to continue to press in to Jesus, the author and finisher of our faith. Only He can be your strength as you *become all that you can be for His glory!*

DAILY TIME WITH JESUS

> "Your word is a lamp to my feet and a light for my path."
>
> Psalm 119:105

The bedrock of who I am in Jesus Christ is based on my having a relationship with Him. God is a jealous God! And as my Creator, He desires and requires daily time with me. As women, we are the same way. We desire and require daily time with our husbands, children and friends in order to stay connected. Why should it surprise us that God is the same way? Christianity is the only religion where God wants a loving and intimate relationship with us on an individual basis. And the best part is God is into *all* the little details that we as women love. He created us to love those little details. Think of our conversations with others. We have to tell every little detail to them in order to feel like we have fully conveyed our hearts, even when some of those little details bore them or our husbands.

Look at God's creation around you and observe how the seasons change throughout the year. Right when we are tired of the current weather season, the next weather pattern begins. Notice how much God is into details! God also loves variety and colors and beauty just like we do. Our desire to fill our homes with color and beautiful things and then to change it up again after awhile is all from the Father heart of God.

God designed us as women to be nurturers. This should help us understand the reason why God wants to nurture His relationship with us because He made us in 'His image.' He wants to be intimately involved in our lives. He wants us to share *with Him* all the details that bounce around in our hearts and minds and then to cast those thoughts and cares onto Him. The only way that this can happen is if we make Him a priority and set aside *daily time* with Him. God has so much to offer us, however, many of us never avail ourselves of the intimate relationship He wants to bless us with.

This is the most important *key* to becoming the woman God has planned for each of us to be. We *need* this daily time with Him to help us navigate through the many roads and seasons of life that our womanhood will take us. We have to *decide* here and now that from this day forward we are going to give God our daily attention and stay faithful to that commitment. We must choose to make our relationship with God our number one priority and under that priority everything else will then fall into place. If you think about it, God (our Creator) is the one who is in total control. So why wouldn't we want to turn to Him for our daily guidance and direction through the ups and downs of life?

DAILY READING:

Begin with five minutes a day, then go to ten minutes, and then try fifteen minutes a day. Before you know it, you might be spending one hour or an hour and a half alone with God each day. As you choose to daily spend this time with Him, you will find it will become a need in your life rather than a commitment or duty. Just like your body needs food to sustain itself, your spirit man needs spiritual food to sustain itself in order to grow spiritually? Can you remember what you ate for lunch three days ago, or breakfast five days ago? Maybe if you thought hard you could remember, but what you do know for sure is that the food you ate nourished you. It is the same spiritually. You may not always remember what God feeds you each day, but your spiritual man is nourished and grows from it. Glory to God! He is so faithful!

> "All Scripture is God-breathed and is useful for teaching, rebuking, correcting and training in righteousness, so that the (wo)man of God may be thoroughly equipped for every good work." (Emphasis added)
>
> 2 Timothy 3:16-17

My suggestion is that you go to www.oneyearbibleonline.com and print off the daily readings that they have already organized for you. Choose the version of the Bible that you are most comfortable with, and make the commitment to read through the Bible in one year and do this year after year. I have been doing this since I was a teenager and I learn and grow each year that I read it through again. If you want to highlight verses that minister to you I suggest you use 'Crayola Twistables.' They are pencil-like and do not bleed through to the other side of the page in your Bible. (They also sell the 'One Year Bible' in all the various translations at your local Christian bookstore if you would rather have it already broken up for you.)

(*Time commitment is about fifteen minutes.*)

> "For the word of God is living and active. Sharper than any double-edged sword, it penetrates even to dividing soul and spirit, joints and marrow; it judges the thoughts and attitudes of the heart. Nothing in all creation is hidden from God's sight. Everything is uncovered and laid bare before the eyes of him to whom we must give account."
>
> Hebrews 4:12-13

For the Christian who can handle more, I encourage you to purchase a Bible that has all the commentaries at the bottom of the Scripture passages (such as *Thompson Chain Reference* or the *Life Application Bible* or *The Everyday Life Bible (Amplified Version) with Joyce Meyer Commentary* which is my favorite) and read them along with your daily reading. This gives you even more insight to the texts you read each day, but does take a bit more time. (*Time commitment is about another ten to fifteen minutes.*)

I also encourage you to read a few devotionals each day that are only a few paragraphs long. There are many to choose from at your Christian bookstores. Find a couple that you really like and let them bless you. My personal favorites are: *Streams in the Desert* and *Springs in the Valley* by Mrs. Charles E. Cowman; *My Utmost for His Highest* and *Daily Thoughts for Disciples* by Oswald Chambers; and *God's Best Secrets* by Andrew Murray.

'Women of Faith' also publishes yearly devotionals that are always good and *Our Daily Bread* is another great monthly publication. (*Time commitment is about ten to fifteen minutes.*)

As a busy wife, home school mom, homemaker, and now daycare provider, I wanted to read all the Christian books I could, but didn't see where I could find the chunks of time to accomplish that desire. So I came up with the idea of incorporating them into my quiet time. I would add one or two of these kinds of books at a time and read a page or a section or a chapter of each book daily. Then I was actually finishing books in about thirty to sixty days. But I was getting them read and gleaning from them! I love reading books from all of "the old dead guys." Books like "Absolute Surrender" by Andrew Murray and Hannah Hurnard's "Hinds Feet in High Places" are *must-reads*. Andrew Murray has written twenty to thirty books and they are all excellent. You can also find great titles from authors like C.S. Lewis, Watchman Nee, and R.A. Torrey. I also love reading contemporary authors like Jack Hayford, Jimmy Evans, Robert Morris, Jim Cymbala, Chuck Swindoll, John Bevere, James Dobson, Joyce Meyer, all the Women of Faith speakers, and many more. I like to use a post-it note to mark my place in these books. They have great re-sticking power. For the younger, technological generations, most of these books and the One Year Bible can also be set up and read on your computer.

(*Time commitment is about fifteen to thirty minutes depending on what portion size you decide to read.*)

Mostly I start my day spending time with the Lord in the early morning which means I adjust my bedtime to get the sleep I require so I can meet with God. When I was younger I often spent time with Him before bed. Now that my day begins so early, I sometimes spend my time with the Lord prior to bed for the next day's reading. I want God to always be my first priority! By reading ahead, I feel like I am showing Him He *is* still my first priority and to avoid rushing through my 'quiet time' the following morning. Because once the workday begins…it is hard to have that 'precious focused time' with Him. When things in life take over I will find other time openings in my day to spend my time with Him. I encourage you to have a time of day you consistently spend with Him because consistent schedules help us succeed. But don't feel bound to it either if things come up. *What matters is that you spend time with Him.* Just like sometimes our husbands or friends wait for our free time to be given to them, God understands those crazy days and patiently waits for you. Just make that the exception, not the rule as you make your time with God a priority.

> "How can a young man keep his way pure? By living according to your word. I seek you with all my heart; do not let me stray from your commands. I have hidden your word in my heart that I might not sin against you. Praise be to you, O Lord; teach me your decrees. With my lips I recount all the laws that come from your mouth. I rejoice in following your statutes as one rejoices in great riches. I meditate on

your precepts and consider your ways. I delight in your decrees; I will not neglect your word."

Psalm 119:9-16

DAILY PRAYER:

George Mueller lived in the 1800's and was an incredible man of God. He was a man full of faith and prayer. God asked him to open up a place for orphan children to go to since there was very little provision for the orphans at that time in history. George believed that if God asked him to provide for these orphans, then God would be the provider for them through prayer. George never asked man for money or provision. He only asked God to meet the daily needs through people, but God would be the one who would cause the people to give money...not George. God DID provide! The orphanage continued to grow in size over the years which meant the needed provision grew as well. God was faithful through it all. I share this story with you to help you understand who George Mueller was so you will appreciate what he had to say on the topic of prayer. *"I began to meditate on the New Testament from the beginning, early in the morning. The first thing I did, after having asked in a few words for the Lord's blessing upon His precious Word, was to begin to meditate on the Word of God, searching as it were every verse to get a blessing out of it, not for the sake of the public ministry of the Word, not for the sake of preaching upon what I had meditated upon, but for obtaining food for my own soul. The result I have found to be almost invariably this, that after a few minutes my soul has been led to confession, or to thanksgiving, or to intercession (praying for others), or to supplication (to make humble requests to God); so that, though I did not as it were give myself to prayer, but to meditation (focused thinking on God), yet it turned almost immediately more or less into prayer. When thus I have been for a while making confession or intercession or supplication, or have given thanks, I go on to the next words or verse, turning all as I go on into prayer for myself or others as the Word may lead to it, but still continually keeping before me that food for my own soul is the object of my meditation. Formerly I often spent a quarter of an hour, or half an hour, or even an hour on my knees, before being conscious of having derived comfort, encouragement, humbling of soul, and often, after having suffered much from wandering of mind for the first ten minutes, or a quarter of an hour, or even half an hour, I only then began to really pray. I scarcely ever suffer now in this way; for my heart being nourished by the truth, being brought into experimental fellowship with God, I speak to my Father and to my Friend about the things that He has brought before me in His precious Word. It often now astonishes me that I did not sooner see this point."*—George Mueller's Secret

If you have a chance, research George Mueller and you will be encouraged and amazed at how God worked in his life through prayer.

In *Daily Thoughts for Disciples* Oswald Chambers says: *"When we pray we give God a chance to work in the unconscious realm of the lives of those for whom we pray. When we come into the secret place it is the Holy Spirit's passion for souls that is at work, not our passion, and He can work through us as He likes."* Have you ever had a dream about someone or thought of someone without having seen them in awhile? This is the Holy Spirit asking you to lift them up in prayer. Also when people ask you to pray for them, please take the time to pray, especially if you told them you would.

As we get closer to people, we begin to see the areas in their lives that they struggle with. *These insights into their lives are not for us to judge them, but for us to know better how to pray for them.*

Psalm 46:10 "Be still, and know that I am God; I will be exalted among the nations, I will be exalted in the earth." Part of prayer is being still and silent before God. In his book, *God's Best Secrets*, Andrew Murray says, *"When we pray, we think we know well enough how to speak to God. And we forget that one of the very first things in prayer is to be silent before God, so that He may reveal Himself. By His hidden but mighty power, God will manifest His presence, resting on us and working in us. To know God in the personal experience of His presence and love is life indeed."* After we have been still and silent for awhile, we need to ask God, *"What do you want to speak to me today?"* Then we need to listen and see if the Holy Spirit gives us an impression, verses from Scripture, a picture-thought, a song, or words from the heart of God for us. You'll be amazed at how He will do this if you give Him the opportunity. Andrew Murray also says: *"Just as the sun rising each morning is the pledge of light throughout the day, so the quiet time of waiting upon God, yielding ourselves to Him to shine on us, will be the pledge of His presence and His power abiding with us all day long."* Psalm 4:6b-7a "Let the light of your face shine upon us, O Lord. You have filled my heart with greater joy."

We need to give each day to God and ask Him to order our steps and arrange any divine appointments He has for us to encourage or minister to another person. This means we are asking God to allow us to be a part of His business rather than saying we want Him to be a part of our busyness. We can also ask Him to wake us up at a certain time in the morning so we can have our "time with Him." Try it and see all the creative ways He will wake you up to keep that commitment with Him. You'll be surprised and blessed!

Another great thing about the Holy Spirit is He can help me remember things. When I am flustered and unable to write something down, I ask Him to remind me of it later when I need to remember it. When I've been in a real time crunch I have even asked God to help me with a parking place or a short line in the grocery store. *Prayer is our link to communicate with our Creator who loves us and cares about every detail of our lives.*

> "Nevertheless, I will bring health and healing to it; I will heal my people and will let them enjoy abundant peace and security."
>
> Jeremiah 33:6

> "But he was pierced for our transgressions, he was crushed for our iniquities; the punishment that brought us peace was on him, and by his wounds we are healed."
>
> Isaiah 53:05

You can also pray by faith for daily healings of sicknesses or ailments that afflict you or your family or friends. Believe in faith and command the healing to take place in the name of Jesus which is the name that holds the power of healing. John 14:14 "You may ask me for anything in my Name, and I will do it." Be specific as you pray. An example would be: "In Jesus Name, I command healing to my sore throat. I command the swelling in my throat to go down and my immune system to rise to the occasion and fight off the sickness in my body. Amen!" It blesses God when we exercise our faith in every way. It shows Him that we believe and trust in Him for every thing in our lives.

We can ask God for heart desires that we have ranging from things, to life events or desired accomplishments to come to pass. As long as we pray with the right motives of humility and trust of His ultimate will to be done, it is amazing to see Him answer prayers. Psalm 37:4 "Take delight in the Lord, and He will give you the desires of your heart." A lot of the furniture in my home I prayed and asked God for. When money was tight it was usually given to me or found somewhere. The key is to be willing to wait for Him to answer. I wanted a green loveseat for our bedroom and while at a community garage sale this green loveseat was on a lawn with a sign on it that said: FREE! Our fake Christmas tree was getting old and falling apart. We had even used cement at the unstable base to make the stand last a little longer. I asked the Lord to replace it during a time of low funds. My son was working for a moving company and came home with a free tree someone could not fit on the truck and said he could have. It was the nicest fake Christmas tree we have ever owned.

When our income became better I was looking for used leather couches to replace our cloth set that had lasted for 10 years. I was willing to buy used ones for the right price but God showed us an opportunity to buy new ones for an incredible price. God works according to our current set of circumstances. I have prayed for my shy son to overcome his shyness to become the man of God He was destined to become and those prayers have been answered. I prayed for the traits in my husband and am thankful for him as the answer to prayer. I have prayed for strength or wisdom to fulfill an overwhelming set of responsibilities or to grow in an area in my life that needs maturing. Whatever it is, we don't have to do it alone! God wants to be included in every part of the process. He is only a prayer away.

> "In the same way, the Spirit helps us in our weakness. We do not know what we ought to pray for, but the Spirit himself intercedes for us with groans that words cannot express. And he who searches our hearts knows the mind of the Spirit, because the Spirit intercedes for the saints in accordance with God's will."
>
> Romans 8:26-27

As we keep an open line of communication with God throughout the day, and make God a priority in our lives, we become a conduit for the Holy Spirit to pray through us prayers we don't even know that our spirit man is praying. Sometimes the deep concerns of our lives make it hard for us to put our prayers into words. Know that the Holy Spirit is praying through you the cries of your heart as well as what He wants to pray through you, His willing servant.

JOURNAL KEEPING:

I really encourage you to have a journal. In it you can put the prayer requests that you want to pray for daily and you can also write the date of when those prayers were answered. Of course, some prayers never go away like: praying for our husbands, children, pastor, church, friends etc. Use your journal to vent your feelings to the Lord. *It is very therapeutic to write it all out to Him in prayer and leave it at His feet.* Write in your journal verses that stick out to you during your Bible reading time or things you've read in your devotionals or the other books you're reading that have touched your heart. You can also look back and see how you've grown in the Lord over time. (*Time commitment is about ten to fifteen minutes or longer if you have a lot on your heart to vent to your heavenly Father.*)

    I have found that when I am going through difficult times, God uses one or more of the things I have read that day to either answer questions I've been asking Him or the words I read became a healing balm on a wound in my heart. Over the years it has amazed me how the words that I read on that particular day were *exactly* what I needed to hear to minister to my spirit and calm my soul (mind, will, and emotions). How

God orchestrated me reading it on that day still amazes me. Once again… *God is in to all the details of each of our lives.* Since we live in the age of everyone having a cell phone and texting, I now store verses and quotes in my phone to read when I need to be encouraged or to use to encourage others.

Lastly, another idea I did for a year was I added an additional evening Scripture reading time with the Lord and used the One Year Bible chronological schedule. It is set up to read the Bible in the historically chronological order of biblical events. For example, you would read the same parable in all four gospels in one sitting. Very interesting! I was richly blessed by beginning and ending my days with the Word of God. (*This is about a fifteen minute time commitment.*)

Well, woman of God…are you ready to step out in faith and commit yourself to the author and lover of your spirit, soul and body? He is waiting for you!

I, _____,
commit today to spending daily time with my Creator who loves me intimately and cares about all the little details of my life. I commit to pray, journal and include God in all the daily concerns of my life.

Date: _____

WEEKLY CHURCH ATTENDANCE:

The other commitments that will propel you into being a Godly woman are faithful church attendance and involvement in that church body. We are always learning more of who God is. We will never arrive at a full understanding of Him until we are with Him in eternity and He transforms our minds completely. In God's plan, the church is designed as a place for us to rub off on each other. We get to grow from one another's experiences. We get to practice Christ-likeness and the fruit of the Spirit on each other. Like a diamond with its multiple facets, we get to see the many facets of who God is in each individual we meet there. "As iron sharpens iron so one man sharpens another." Proverbs 27:17 We get to rejoice with those who rejoice and mourn with those who mourn. We get to: DO LIFE TOGETHER! Don't miss out on this opportunity to be in the lives of other people and let other people be in your life. This is one of the ways we get to be 'Jesus with skin on.' *We must be* purposeful *about growing in our relationship with God!*

I, _____,
commit to consistently attend a local church body and get involved in relationships with fellow believers and to serve the local church with my abilities and giftings.

Date: _____

ALWAYS PUT GOD FIRST AND MAKE
HIM THE PRIORITY IN YOUR LIFE!

GOD'S WILL FOR MY LIFE

> "And without faith it is impossible to please God, because anyone who comes to him must believe that he exists and that he rewards those who earnestly seek him."
>
> Hebrews 11:6

Because God cares about you in every way, His will for your life is to have an intimate relationship with Him as your Father. God created us and knows how each of us is bent. He gave us our personalities, talents, and giftings. He wants to help us discover how to use what He has given us for His glory. Psalm 139:13 "For you created my inmost being; you knit me together in my mother's womb." As we walk the road of life we begin to realize what our heart desires are because we are each uniquely made. I know that for me my heart was always inclined to being a wife and mother, and to someday to be a pastor's wife. God birthed those things in my heart as a young teenager and I prepared myself for those roles as I walked through life.

> "Delight yourself in the Lord and he will give you the desires of your heart. Commit your way to the Lord; trust in him and he will do this: He will make your righteousness shine like the dawn, the justice of your cause like the noonday

sun. Be still before the Lord and wait patiently for him…"

Psalm 37:4-7a

What does it mean to "delight yourself in the Lord and He will give you the desires of your heart?" The Hebrew definition of the word "give" means "to set" or "to put." It means that as we choose to make God a priority in our lives and allow Him to change us from the inside out, then our desires change to align with God's desires for us. This is a lifelong process and we are usually not even aware that it is happening. As we commit our way to the Lord, we begin to align our life decisions and prayers according to His divine will for us.

> "If you remain in me and my words remain in you, ask whatever you wish, and it will be given to you. This is to my Father's glory, that you bear much fruit, showing yourselves to be my disciples."

John 15:7-8

I was blessed to grow up in a Christian home because my dad, Donald Hill, chose to make Jesus the Lord of his life and start a new lineage of Christians in his family line. Dad was born into a family where his father was an alcoholic who abandoned his family when my father was a young boy. My Gramie, dad's mom, raised her two sons as a single mom for many years before God blessed her with a good husband when the boys were young teenagers. Then my dad had a brain tumor at sixteen years old and they just happened to live near one of the best brain surgeons in the country at the time…which was really God at work. The surgery was a success (or I wouldn't be here), but dad was left with seizures. This left him with some emotional issues and confusion that landed him in juvenile hall. While there, my dad was given a New Testament and devoured the book of John. At this juncture in his life he made a serious re-commitment to God. Dad had received the free gift of salvation that Jesus offers each one of us when he was twelve years old, but he didn't grow much in his faith at that time in his life. (As a young boy he used to baptize his brother and cousin in the pond on his granddad's property in Texas.) In the end the brain tumor was the tool God used to lead my Gramie back to God as well. After my father re-connected with God he felt God calling him to become a minister of the gospel of Christ and went to Bible College where he met my mom, got married and then went on to seminary. So I was blessed to grow up as a pastor's kid and later on a missionary's kid. Both of my parents felt the call to the mission field in the 1980's, but the mission board wouldn't accept my dad due to his seizures. They feared that he would have limited access to his medication and did not want that responsibility on their shoulders. But my parents knew that God had put that call on their lives. So they prayed to God that if He indeed wanted them to go to the mission field then He needed to heal my dad of his seizures. And God did! My parents served as missionaries in the Philippines for ten years. I wasn't even aware that my dad used to have seizures until we were in the Philippines and he and I were talking and he told me about it. I never remember seeing him have one. The four years of being the daughter of a pastor and the four years I was in the Philippines before going to college totally shaped who I am today. That cross-cultural experience broadened my perspective on life and people and helped me understand how blessed we really are in America. All of those experiences also birthed in my heart the desire to be in full-time ministry as an adult.

Since I grew up in the church, I knew all the Bible stories, but I still didn't know how to be personally intimate with God until I ran into a Filipino man, named Joel who served under "Youth with a Mission." Joel had not grown up in a Christian home and had experienced the drug and sex scene, but he was more "on fire" for God than I was. This challenged me to kick my relationship with God into a higher gear. I began reading the Bible myself and was amazed with all that it said. I began devouring the teachings of Jesus and applying them to my life. Then I became "on fire" for God too as my relationship with Him became my own; my intimate connection with Him had begun.

I am the oldest of three girls in our family. I was seventeen years old during my parent's one year furlough and at the end of their furlough I stayed in the U.S. to start college at eighteen years old while my family went back to the Philippines. Gramie and I even drove them to the airport which was hard. Then my Aunt and I dropped off Gramie at the airport to fly back to her home in Texas, and then she drove me to college and dropped me off. That was a bit scary at the time.

During my junior year of college, I met my husband, Gary Hicks. God had placed in each of our hearts the various qualities that we had desired in a spouse and we were a perfect match. We both also wanted to have four children.

Since I knew that God cares about all the little details I cared about, I prayed for the gender of each of our kids. I prayed for a girl first because I only had sisters and thought I should start with something I was more familiar with. I asked for her to have blonde hair and blue eyes and for her to have the long, dark eyelashes that I had always wanted. Rebekah was born a toe-head with blue eyes and dark eye lashes. I have blue eyes, but Gary has brown eyes and darker features so I assumed this would be a difficult task for God based on the BB, Bb, bb, scientific formula. In my immaturity I shared this desire with Gary before we were married and that night he had a prophetic dream and saw a blonde haired, blue-eyed little girl walking in the middle of each of us holding our hands. That silliness in my heart, God honored with a prophetic dream. What God already knew, but Gary and I would not find out for 16 more years, was that his real heritage was from Spain with the blue eyes hiding in his genetics. Since Gary was adopted some of his true origins were still a blur at this time. God sees and knows what we do not.

Then I felt the courage to have a boy and asked God for a boy next, with light-colored eyes, and dark eyelashes. Joshua was born with blue (turned green) eyes and dark eyelashes. I also asked God for two-three year age gaps because I felt that I needed that amount of time between kids in order to care well for each child. Bekah and Josh are two and a half years apart.

Next, I asked God for a girl, but she came a little earlier than I thought I was ready for. Joshua and Rachel are both May babies, two years apart. I had just gotten Joshua off of the bottle when I found out I was pregnant with Rachel. I didn't feel I was ready to be pregnant again. I remember going to my first appointment and they did an inner sonogram. I saw her heart beating and surrendered to God and cried all the way home thanking Him for another child. I asked for her to be a girl and to have blue/green eyes and dark eyelashes which she has.

After three kids we were tired and considered being done. We even tried to sell our baby stuff at a garage sale. It didn't sell, though. Then about six months later we again had the desire to have our fourth child. We got pregnant and I prayed that it would be a boy. I didn't pray that he have light colored eyes or light colored hair because God had already answered that prayer for three of our kids and I thought it would only be fair if one of our kids had Gary's brown eyes and brown hair. So James was born with brown eyes and brown hair and we call him Gary's twin, thirty-three years apart. Rachel and James are three years apart.

I shared all this with you to kind of show the process of walking through the progression of finding the will of God. I believe that as I put God first in my life, my heart's desires lined up with His divine plan. Then my prayers to Him began to align with His will also. As I prayed, what I was praying for was answered because they were the heart's desires that God had put in my heart. He answered my prayers accordingly because they were originally from His heart first. I always hesitate telling these stories because to the human mind, these are stupid, unimportant details to pray about. *But the truth is our loving, heavenly Father wants each of us to have a simple, child-like faith.*

A similar process happened with the seed God put in my heart to be a pastor's wife. After Gary and my dating relationship began to get serious, I told him about my desire to be a pastor's wife. He chuckled inside because he had no intention of heading down that path. He knew that he would serve God in the Christian school system, where he was working when we met, but he had no desire at that time to be a pastor even though he had already had a "prophetic word" spoken over him when he was a teen about becoming a pastor someday. God had definitely orchestrated all the details of our becoming husband and wife. So I just left that seed in my heart and waited.

We began by serving in various ways as volunteers at every church we attended in our early years together. We served on the worship team, taught Sunday-School, worked in the nursery; Gary served as an elder and even as youth pastor for a season. For the first thirteen years of our marriage God was training and grooming us through our service in the church. God was preparing us through ministry life experiences for "His call" on our lives. During this time God began birthing the desire to pastor in my husband's heart. It was a beautiful thing! At this juncture, Gary was blessed with the opportunity to work at a wonderful church where he held many different positions and gleaned from each experience how to become a better pastor. We served there seven years: three and a half years as volunteer leaders and three and a half years as a staff pastor. We were able to experience the growth of that church from nine hundred people to four thousand people and all the changes that go with it.

Then the surprise came for both of us. We were both content with the role of associate pastor, but God had other plans. Through very interesting circumstances, God called us out of California where we had spent our entire marriage to come to North Texas to plant a church. Gary had no desire to be a senior pastor and wrestled with God for six weeks over the call to do so. He even experienced pain in his hip area while he wrestled with God just like Jacob did in the Bible. I had no desire to start a church from scratch and wrestled with God for a while as well. It has been a hard, seven-year road, but God has been faithful and grown each of us closer to Him thru it all! It has been a process over our twenty-three years of marriage to continuously seek God's plan for our lives and then watch Him orchestrate circumstances accordingly which is how we "live by faith…not by sight."

As you walk 'your road' you need to use prayer, Scripture confirmation, input from others that have a Godly influence in your life, and life circumstances to guide and direct your steps to finding God's will for your life.

> "For I know the plans I have for you," declares the Lord, "plans to prosper you and not to harm you, plans to give you hope and a future. Then you will call upon me and come and pray to me, and I will listen to you. You will seek me and find me when you seek me with all your heart. I will be found by you," declares the Lord.
>
> God's direct promise to us in Jeremiah 29:11-14a

PURSUE GOD WITH YOUR WHOLE HEART, AND HE WILL FULFILL ALL THE DESIRES THAT HE HAS PLACED THERE!

LEARN YOURSELF

For some reason, as women, we expect our husbands and/or friends to totally understand us and know why we do what we do, and why we think what we think. Now, let's be truthful here. How can we have that expectation on them and not have the same expectation on ourselves?

I believe that we, as women, are quite complicated. But God made us this way and He wants to help us to learn ourselves. We need to take every opportunity to think about and pray through why we think or feel what we think or feel and why we do what we do. *We need to know ourselves.*

We need to decide what we believe and why we believe it. We need to explore the root reasons as to why our emotions flare up when they do. We need to know our bodies and our cycles which will help us to understand our mood fluctuations. As we face our thoughts and feelings we can then make wiser decisions on how we respond to others. For example, if it is the time of month when my hormones are in full swing, I believe it is my job to be aware of that and keep my mouth SHUT. I am not in a rational state of mind at that time and my emotions are not trustworthy. I don't believe I have the right to take out my confused emotions on my family or friends. Usually, at those times, we have no idea why we feel the way we do, we just feel that way. This is your clue to just keep your mouth shut and if possible, escape from others until you feel under control again. This is also what I have taught our two daughters as they have entered womanhood.

This process of learning yourself is life-long and is accomplished as you daily spend time with your Creator. Only He can help you understand who you really are because you are *His unique design*. He wants to walk you through the steps of:

- Setting you free from lies by teaching you His *truth*.

- Bringing you healing from the present hurts you are walking through by teaching you how to forgive and love like He did and does.

- Revealing what He desires to 'heal' deep within you from your past in order to clean out the skeletons in the closets of your soul. He will challenge you to face them head on and deal with them.

- Know that He is gentle and loving and His timing for the cleaning of each area in your life is impeccable.

As you continue to get to know God you will be intrigued with the various circumstances He uses to help you to heal or become mature in Him. These circumstances usually involve pain because pain motivates us to change. We rarely grow or change when things are "status-quo." You must understand that "*God never wastes our pain!*" He will always use it for His glory and for your healing if you allow Him to. Take advantage of your time of getting ready in the morning and getting ready for bed at night by spending time thinking and praying through the issues that God is currently dealing with you on. You can also use drive time, lunch-time, or waiting in the car time to your advantage as well. God loves to correct our 'stinking-thinking.'

The last thing we need to master is often very hard for women because we are usually where the buck stops. "Nothing gets done unless Mama had a hand in it, right?" Well, Mama, you need to know your limitations. This is so important. If you are over-extended and burnt out, then where will your family and the household be? You have to pace yourself and set healthy boundaries that fit your personality and abilities. Only as you know yourself can you begin to do this. When unavoidable circumstances force you to push yourself really hard, you need to be sure that you have time to recover from it after your commitment is fulfilled. This will help you to avoid depression or sickness.

The best part about learning yourself is you can clearly share who you "really" are with your spouse or friends in a way that is healthy and LIFE-GIVING. Neither your husband nor your friends are mind readers and we should not put that expectation on them. As you begin to truly know yourself then you can better communicate your needs, wants, desires, and dreams with your loved ones in a healthy way and do "your part" in becoming a healthy communicator. Most husbands want to meet our needs…they just don't know what our needs are. As we remove the guessing game for them, we increase their odds of success. Of course, there are selfish husbands out there who have no desire to meet your needs or you may be a single parent. Then you need to know that your God wants to be a husband to you. He is a perfect husband! Read Song of Solomon and view yourself as the bride and God as the groom. God is a faithful husband and He will NEVER ABANDON YOU!

Always remember that every one of us has days of victory and days of failure, but "His mercies are new every morning." Lamentations 3:23 Whenever we mess up we can always start fresh again tomorrow, with Him. Praise God! He is so good to us!

BOTTOM LINE: BE WHO GOD
MADE YOU TO BE!
BECOME WHO GOD PREDESTINED
YOU TO BECOME!
YOU ARE *GOD'S UNIQUE WOMAN!*

MAKE YOURSELF A PRIORITY TOO!

> "Do you not know that in a race all the runners run, but only one gets the prize? Run in such a way as to get the prize. Everyone who competes in the games goes into strict training. They do it to get a crown that will not last; but we do it to get a crown that will last forever. Therefore I do not run like a man running aimlessly; I do not fight like a man beating the air. No, I beat my body and make it my slave so that after I have preached to others, I myself will not be disqualified for the prize."
>
> I Corinthians 9:24-27

For some reason, we as women, put ourselves last on the totem pole of life. Usually by the time we get to the end of that pole we are totally out of energy. This mentality is wrong and will not help you finish the race well. We think about and provide everything that our husbands and kids need to thrive, but for some reason we think that meeting our needs is less important. We often lie to ourselves and believe in error, that we "will" have energy when it becomes time to meet our needs… but we rarely do. We have to change our thinking today! This is *not* a sprint; this is a *marathon*. I want you to win your marathon with energy to spare!

We need to make ourselves and our needs a priority. How many of us stay-at-home moms never get to take a shower or get out of our comfortable, ratty pajamas? How many of us only wear a pony tail, day in and day out because it is quick and easy? How many of us think that we can only have hobbies before children or after they are grown? How many of us working women feel like the daily grind never ends? How many of us believe exercise is walking up and down the stairs of our house? These are all lies that keep us trapped into feeling depressed, overwhelmed, or like a failure.

Ladies, it is time to make yourself a priority too! We have to be pro-active in this area in order to maintain a healthy self-esteem. *Remember, we are setting the example of healthy living in front of our children day in and day out.* Whatever you did to make yourself feel pretty before the kids came, you *need* to keep doing. You need to find a flattering hairstyle that is easy to maintain and if you wore make-up when you lured your husband into your life, then continue to wear it. It is not fair to our husbands to stop making ourselves look pretty after the kids come. We want them to take good care of themselves too, right? We can't have that expectation of them, yet have a different expectation of ourselves. You need to shower daily and wear pretty clothes that make you feel good about yourself. I know that having babies usually causes extra weight gain that comes on easier than it goes off, but you still need to find clothes that feel good and flatter the figure you do have so that you feel good about yourself.

Get creative with your exercising and only bite off an exercise program that you know you can chew. While your kids are little you can push them in strollers on walks or you can do video exercise in your home while they nap or are sitting in a playpen or swing etc. They can watch you and be entertained. When the kids get older, go on bike rides or walks together or whatever else is a fit for your family. *Exercise makes you feel healthy and good about your self.* We all know how necessary and beneficial exercise is to our health. This is another area of discipline like our daily time with God. You have to first make the choice to exercise. Then explore your options to find out which type of exercise will keep your interest. Have alternative exercise options as well because after awhile everything gets boring and repetitious. Start with once a week and continue to increase the frequency in your exercise program to three to five times per week, twenty to thirty minutes per day. Every one has different expectations on themselves in this area. For most of us, exercise is not something we love to do. But we do love the way it makes us feel afterwards. It is exciting to feel your heart muscle strengthen as you do a cardio workout. It is rewarding to feel your muscles start to re-shape your frame as you faithfully lift weights. (The studies say that lifting weights helps to prevent osteoporosis. None of us want to have brittle bones as an older woman.) We may not always lose weight from our endeavors, but we will see our bodies become more tone and fit and we will feel healthier. Weight gain has always been a struggle for me. Be encouraged that this is a constant battle for most of us. You are not alone.

If you already have hobbies then make the time to do them. If you don't have any hobbies then explore until you find some. At least once a month enjoy a hobby or time with your girlfriends. The duties of marriage, motherhood, and work should not strip you of your individual identity and recreation. We need to maintain a healthy balance in every area of our lives.

> AS YOU SPEND TIME WITH GOD DAILY... AND TAKE SNIPPETS OF TIME FROM YOUR DAY TO MEET YOUR NEEDS, YOU WILL STAY HEALTHY EMOTIONALLY AND PHYSICALLY. THEN YOU CAN PASS ALONG THAT HEALTH TO YOUR FAMILY AND LOVED ONES WHO INTERACT WITH YOU ALL THE TIME.

WE'RE IN A WAR!

> "So, if you think you are standing firm, be careful that you don't fall! No temptation has seized you except what is common to man. And God is faithful; he will not let you be tempted beyond what you can bear. But when you are tempted, he will also provide a way out so that you can stand up under it."
>
> I Corinthians 10:12-13

Now more than ever, we are in a war against good and evil; God and Satan. The good news is that we know God is the final victor, but the battle is still raging. Our culture is lowering its standards of morality daily and it is done in such a slow yet sly way, that many Christians aren't even aware that they are being affected by it.

We have to protect our minds and our hearts from the lies that the enemy has flooded our world with today. Only as we wash our minds with the truth of the Word of God can we even begin to fight the battle of right and wrong. The old children's song I grew up singing was: "Oh, be careful little eyes what you see. Oh, be careful little ears what you hear. Oh, be careful little mouth what you say. Oh, be careful little hands what you do. For the Father up above is looking down in love." I John 2:15-17 "Do not love the world or anything in the world. If anyone loves the world, the love of the Father is not in him. For everything in the world—the cravings of sinful man, the lust of his eyes and the boasting of what he has and does—comes not from the Father but from the world. The world and its desires pass away, but the man who does the will of God lives forever."

We have to *proactively protect* our minds from the things we watch on TV and movies. We must protect our thought life in the books we read and the music we listen to. Most of what the world has to offer will fill our minds with the illusion that money, sex, and power bring fulfillment and that "I am number one" and "selfishness is good." These lies of Satan are berating us through our culture and unless we realize we are in a battle and begin to fight back with truth from God's Word, I fear we will be deeply wounded in the war. John 17:14-18 says: "I have given them your word and the world has hated them, for they are not of the world any more than I am of the world. My prayer is not that you take them out of the world but that you protect them from the evil one. They are not of the world, even as I am not of it. Sanctify them by the truth; your word is truth. As you sent me into the world, I have sent them into the world." Satan's goal is to destroy all of us. He mostly does it through the lies he gets us to believe that we hear through the media. Media teaches us that marriage is not a forever commitment and being a single parent is easy and men are less smart than women are. It teaches us to always look for something better when things get tough because the grass is always greener elsewhere. These are all *lies* sent from the pit of hell to destroy us! Satan's goal is to destroy marriages, which then destroys the children, which then destroys society. It is a domino affect of destruction and it is very, very effective. Hebrews 5:13-14 "Anyone who lives on milk, being still an infant, is not acquainted with the teaching about righteousness. But solid food is for the mature, who by constant use have trained themselves to distinguish good from evil."

I Corinthians 10:23-24 "Everything is permissible"—but not everything is beneficial. "Everything is permissible"—but not everything is constructive. Nobody should seek his own good, but the good of others." For the Christians who are aware of the obvious lies of Satan, I now want to challenge you with one of his sneaky tricks: extra-curricular activities and busyness. Families today believe that in order for their kids to be well-rounded and get into college they have to be in multiple extra-curricular activities. They also believe that in order for their child to get a college sports scholarship they need to have their child in that sport year-round, year after year. The truth is that the money that is spent on all the sports fees, gas to and from the sports events, and fast-food during the busyness could be saved and set aside for college instead. Then there would be more time to spend on our relationship with God and our family. I am not against these activities, but we have to keep it all in balance. If these activities are preventing your family from sitting down to have dinner together or from ever having "down time," then those activities are in control of your life rather than enhancing your kid's lives. Just like adults…kids need "*down time.*" Kids need unorganized play time so they can be creative and enjoy playing with the neighbor kids. This used to be common in America, but it no longer is. Between all the homework that teachers pile on their students and extra-curricular activities, our kids have joined the "rat race" that the adults are already in and they get to enjoy less of their childhood. Childhood is the only time in life when we can be more "carefree" and not worry about everything the adults have to worry about. I fear we are taking that privilege away from our kids and entering them into our stressed-out world before they even enter adulthood. Matthew 10:16 says: "I am sending you out like sheep among wolves. Therefore be as shrewd as snakes and as innocent as doves." As we bring these areas back into balance we will have a much easier time spending time daily with God, learning ourselves, and will also have the little extra time needed to make ourselves a priority.

One of the Ten Commandments is: Exodus 20:3 "You shall have no other gods (idols) before me." An idol can be anything that we consider to be equal to or above God. When we trust in ourselves, our money, or power we are making those things an idol in our lives. Ultimately, all idols will prove worthless and the true God will prevail. As women we can subconsciously make our husband or children into an idol above God. We often don't even realize we have done it. I know that for the first seven years of our marriage my husband and children were little idols in my heart.

The wonderful husband idol: When I was upset about something I would vent to my husband first and then I went to God. I wanted and expected Gary to fix me.

Then there came a time when that began to change. I went to Gary to share my heart and he was sympathetic and supportive about what was upsetting me, but I still left with a heavy heart. So I went to my heavenly Father and shared it all with Him and He lifted the heavy burden I was carrying. *The truth is that our husbands are not designed to lift our burdens. Only God can lift them. Our husbands are designed to walk the road with us, but not to fix us. God fixes us!* From that point on until now, I go to God during my daily time with Him to cast my burden upon Him and to ask Him to fix me. Then I go to my husband, Gary, to share with him what God is doing in my heart. We can share our burdens with our husband before we go to God as long as we don't expect our husband to heal and lift our burden. This is an area of growth that takes time and practice to make a habit in our lives.

The precious/wonderful children idol: I believe the heavy responsibility of raising our children and their helpless dependence on us, in combination with our God-given nurturing nature sets us up for this common mistake. The correct mindset is: *Each of our children belongs to God! We have them on loan for a short period of time.* We are their God-given care givers and trainers to help steward them into mature adulthood.

While we were youth pastors, we took our youth up to Hume Lake Christian Camps in California during the summer. This is when God confronted me about this idol in my life. That particular summer, they were performing a drama about the five missionary men who were killed by the Waodani Indian tribe in the jungles of Ecuador during the 1950's. They have since made a documentary of this true story called: "Beyond the Gates of Splendor" and a movie of it as well called: "End of the Spear." Both of these movies tell this amazing story of Godly, Christian men who sacrificed their lives to share the Gospel with these people. Their unnecessary deaths angered the protective mom in me that felt it was wrong of God to take these fathers from their young children. As the story continued, I learned how God cared for each of those fatherless children and protected them from that devastating loss. This forced me to face the question of whether or not I trusted God with my kids no matter what? I had to decide then and there if they were God's kids, or my kids? I wrestled with Him over all of this during the week we were there. I left camp that week victorious! I gave each of my children back to God. I can now hold them and my husband, Gary out to God with an open hand rather than a clenched fist. It helps us to surrender them to God if we realize that we really can't control everything in their lives anyway. We can't protect them from all harm or force them to make all the right choices.

> LET GOD HAVE CONTROL OF
> YOUR HUSBAND & CHILDREN
> IN YOUR HEART. HE IS ALREADY
> IN CONTROL ANYWAY.

LOVE WITHOUT RESERVE

> "One of the teachers of the law came and heard them debating. Noticing that Jesus had given them a good answer, he asked him, "Of all the commandments, which is the most important?" The most important one" answered Jesus, "is this: 'Hear O Israel, the Lord our God, the Lord is one. Love the Lord your God with all your heart, and with all your soul, and with all your mind and with all your strength. The second is this: 'Love your neighbor as yourself.' There is no commandment greater than these."
>
> Mark 12: 28-31

We have already discussed how to love the Lord our God with all of our heart, soul, mind, and strength. Now we will discuss loving our neighbor as our self. Jesus is different from all other religions in that He teaches us how to love sacrificially and He taught this by example. Everything He asks us to do, He has already done. That is the kind of God I want to serve. Obviously, this is easier said than done. But the key to succeeding at loving unconditionally is to first make the choice to obey how Jesus has taught us to love and secondly to ask the Holy Spirit to help us to do it. We can't love others like this in our own strength. Only by the power of God in control of our lives can we even begin to live a life full of love.

> "A new command I give you: Love one another. As I have loved you, so you must love one another. By this all men will know that you are my disciples, if you love one another."
>
> John 13:34

The Christian life is a process of learning how to love without reserve, knowing that we are risking getting our hearts hurt by our vulnerability. What God has continued to try to develop in me is a very thick skin while maintaining a very tender heart. This concept can only be accomplished through God's help in our lives. Romans 12:9-10 "Love must be sincere. Hate what is evil; cling to what is good. Be devoted to one another in brotherly love. Honor one another above yourselves." Our human wisdom says that if we get hurt we need to protect ourselves and nurse our wounds and allow seeds of bitterness, rejection, or fear to take root in our hearts as a result of that wound. This is not the example Jesus gave us to follow. Jesus was mocked, humiliated, made fun of, betrayed, beaten, rejected, stoned, whipped, and killed on a cross. Why are we then surprised when we experience many of the same things? Because our culture tells us that our "rights" are being violated. Jesus gave up His "rights" so that He could become the substitute sacrifice for *our sins*. Only as we continue to die to our "rights" will the unconditional love of Jesus take root in our hearts and bear beautiful fruit. I John 2:5-6 "But if anyone obeys his word, God's love is truly made complete in him. This is how we know we are in Him: Whoever claims to live in Him must walk as Jesus did." You will begin to see things more from God's perspective. You will be able to look past the offense and see that the individual, who hurt you, lashed out at you from the brokenness and hurt deep within them. *Hurting people…hurt other people!* You will begin to see Jesus birth in you a compassion for them as you see the situation through God's eyes. It is their wounds or insecurities that are motivating their actions toward you. Then God will turn your offense into love-filled prayers for the offender and instill in you a heartfelt desire to love them more.

> "Do not repay anyone evil for evil. Be careful to do what is right in the eyes of everybody. If it is possible, as far as it depends on you, live at peace with everyone. Do not take revenge, my friends, but leave room for God's wrath, for it is written: "It is mine to avenge; I will repay," says the Lord. On the contrary: "If your enemy is hungry, feed him; if he is thirsty, give him something to drink. In doing this, you will heap burning coals on his head. Do not be overcome by evil, but overcome evil with good."
>
> Romans 12:17-21

Another nugget of truth I have learned over the years is I need to love people "where they are at" rather than where I expect them to be. This means that sometimes we have expectations of maturity on people's behavior that they have not yet attained. If what we think they should already know, they still haven't learned, that leaves us with unrealistic expectations. *Everyone is on their own time-table in their walk with God.* Just like we can look back at ourselves one year ago and see how we've grown to be more like Jesus, we must have that same understanding of other people as well. You are accountable for *your* responses, *not theirs*. (This point does not apply to the children that are still under your care. You are accountable to God for their actions until they enter adulthood and you must keep training them.)

> "You have heard that it was said, 'Eye for eye, and tooth for tooth.' But I tell you, do not resist an evil person. If someone strikes you on the right cheek, turn to him the other also. And if someone wants to sue you and take your tunic, let him have your cloak as well. If someone forces you to go one mile, go with him two miles. Give to the one who asks you, and do not turn away from the one who wants to borrow from you."
>
> Matthew 5:38-42

Love is more of an action than a feeling. Love causes us to act through selfless and sacrificial giving to others around us. We begin to serve others with no thought of receiving anything in return. We put the desire of others above our own and find fulfillment as we meet their needs. This is the kind of love God offers to us and what He desires to birth in our lives toward others as we make Him the Lord of our hearts.

"Love is patient, love is kind. It does not envy, it does not boast, it is not proud. It is not rude, it is not self-seeking, it is not easily angered, it keeps no record of wrongs. Love does not delight in evil but rejoices with the truth. It always protects, always trusts, always hopes, and always perseveres. Love never fails."

I Corinthians 13:4-8a

This is a powerful passage in Scripture. How many of us feel like we do not obey even half of what God commands us to do in this area of love. Only God fulfills this definition of love. *Only as we die to ourselves and surrender to God and His ways of doing things in our lives will we begin to resemble this passage in Scripture.* This is a life-long process for all of us and God will forgive us each time we fail if we ask Him to. Keep giving Him territory in your life and you will begin to see these character traits of love shine brightly in your reactions to others. It will amaze you and you will know that you didn't do it…*He did it in you!*

Lastly, if you are not aware of the five love languages, then you need to read the book: "The Five Love Languages" by Gary Chapman. The five love languages are: Physical Touch and Closeness, Quality Time, Acts of Service, Gift-Giving, and Words of Encouragement. His book will help you discover what your number one love language is and what the number one love language of each of your loved ones is. Then you can begin to show love to each of them in their main love language and communicate your love more effectively. We often show love to others in our main love language, but that is not usually the love language of the other person.

HAVE NO REGRETS AS YOU
LOVE OTHERS FOR JESUS!
*YOU WILL RECEIVE YOUR
REWARD IN HEAVEN!*

MUCH GRACE AND FORGIVENESS

"For all have sinned and fall short of the glory of God, and are justified freely by his grace through the redemption that came by Christ Jesus."

Romans 3:23-24

"For if you forgive men when they sin against you, your heavenly Father will also forgive you. But if you do not forgive men their sins, your Father will not forgive your sins."

Matthew 6:14-15

We all need and want much forgiveness and grace which is *unmerited favor*. Often when we think about these twin virtues we only think about receiving them rather than extending forgiveness and grace to others. Why is that? The reason is because…selfishness is a root sin of mankind. No parent has to teach a baby to say 'mine' or 'no!' It is their sin nature they are born with. Luke 6:31 says: "Do to others as you would have them do to you." We have to treat others the way we want to be treated. I say this to our kids every time their sibling spats arise. I ask them, "Is that the way you want to be treated?" Their answer is usually, "No." This applies to marriage as well. If I want to receive grace from Gary then I must give grace. If I am treating my husband the way I want to be treated and he is treating me the way he wants to be treated, then we rarely have anything to fight about. We are putting each other's needs and desires above our own and then meeting them. *We need to mentally put ourselves in the other person's shoes and try to see things from their perspective. This usually fills us with compassion and understanding that we didn't previously have.*

A tool to help us be full of grace for others is to be very observant of their circumstances in order to better understand what difficulties they might be in. As you do this you will begin to see fatigue or frustration and even despair in people's eyes that you never noticed before. Then take the time to share the love of Jesus with a warm, heartfelt smile and if possible give them an encouraging word. Everybody needs that! Be a light for Jesus in a very dark world! When we listen and learn about the hardships others endure, it will give us an "understanding grace" for their mean or difficult behavior.

Our culture teaches us to get even and to get ahead while stepping on others to get there. This is another one of Satan's lies. The most ironic part is that we are proud of ourselves when we do it to others, but we are livid when others do it to us. How is that for logic? That is Satan for you. He twists some truth with untruth and then twists it some more. Because this thinking is so prevalent in our culture today, we have to clean out our wrong thinking with the truth from the Word of God. We want to avenge ourselves for how others have wronged us but vengeance is mine says the Lord.

Romans 12:17-19 "Do not repay anyone evil for evil. Be careful to do what is right in the eyes of everybody. If it is possible, as far as it depends on you, live at peace with everyone. Do not take revenge, my friends, but leave room for God's wrath, for it is written: "It is mine to avenge; I will repay," says the Lord." We may or may not see it during our time here on earth, but His promise to avenge us will be kept.

It helps if we understand that forgiveness is more for us than it is for the other person. What? That doesn't make any sense! But most of God's ways don't make logical sense to us. As we choose to step out in faith and obey God by forgiving the one who hurt us, then we are set FREE from that bondage of anger and frustration! The way to accomplish this is to ask God to change your heart-feelings toward that person and fill you with His forgiveness toward them. Admit that you don't want to forgive them, yet you want to obey God. Then ask God to change your feelings toward them and help you to forgive them. *You will be amazed how God loves to answer that simple prayer.* Your heart will begin to change and you will have God's love and compassion for that person instead of unforgiveness. Studies have been done which show that bitterness and unforgiveness hurt "our" bodies and make "us" ill. It does not hurt the other person, especially if they don't even know how we feel or don't care that they hurt us. It has been said that bitterness and unforgiveness are a poison that is meant for our enemy, but we are the ones who drink of its fruit. Take back that 'territory' in your mind/heart and be FREE!

> Then Peter came to Him and said, "Lord, how often shall my brother sin against me, and I forgive him? Up to seven times?" Jesus said to him, "I do not say to you, up to seven times, but up to seventy times seven."
>
> Matthew 18:21-22 (NKJV)

This is a frustrating passage of Scripture because it teaches us that we have to keep forgiving others up to 490 times for the *same offense*. I remember how God used a certain woman in my church to teach me how to apply this to my life. This woman just didn't like me. I don't know what I did that made her treat me so poorly, but her true feelings were obvious in her actions. For four years I had to keep forgiving her and give her a clean slate in our relationship. Toward the end of that four years we were participating in a "secret sisters" gift-giving among the women in the church and guess whose name I drew…hers. God challenged me to be extra nice and generous to her and apply another Bible verse to my life. Romans 12:20 "On the contrary: "If your enemy is hungry, feed him; if he is thirsty, give him something to drink. In doing this, you will heap burning coals on his head." I made it my goal to bless her socks off in obedience to this teaching from the Bible. When the time came to reveal who our secret sisters were, she was so shocked and amazed that it was me. From that point on, I didn't have any more issues with her.

We also need to understand that repentance and penitence are not the same. Penitence is feeling sorrow for having committed sins or misdeeds or regret for getting caught. Repentance goes one step further of *turning away from sin and changing our ways.* We must acknowledge that giving and receiving forgiveness is based on the understanding that God, Himself is a JUST God. Because He is JUST, He is fair and impartial and morally correct. Therefore, we can trust that it is He who will justify and sort out our situation in His own time and way.

Here are some key points to help you understand more fully what forgiveness means:

1. Forgiveness is an act of faith toward God.
2. Forgiveness is a dismissal of debt that releases resentment.
3. Forgiveness surrenders the individual's right to extract punishment for the injustice done.
4. Forgiveness is a choice, not a feeling.
5. Forgiveness is not an excuse for the wrong or a denial of judgment for the wrong that was done.
6. Forgiveness transfers the penalty and the determination of the sentence to God.
7. Forgiveness does not require the individual to become a doormat or a martyr.
8. Forgiveness has nothing to do with fairness.
9. Forgiveness is a doorway to reconciliation.

These points are from a book by June Hunt, *How to Forgive When you Don't Feel Like It,*

Harvest House Publishers, Eugene, Oregon; www.harvesthousepublishers.com.

As we obey God in the area of forgiveness and grace we are then able to stay emotionally healthy. As we stay emotionally healthy, we can pass on emotional health to all of the loved ones and friends in our lives.

> OBEY GOD IN THIS AREA AND TRUST
> THE HOLY SPIRIT TO COMPLETE HIS
> DEEP WORK OF FILLING YOU WITH
> HIS FORGIVENESS AND GRACE.

WE'RE ALL UNIQUE! SO DON'T JUDGE!

"Do not judge, or you too will be judged. For in the same way you judge others, you will be judged, and with the measure you use, it will be measured to you. Why do you look at the speck of sawdust in your brother's eye and pay no attention to the plank in your own eye? How can you say to your brother, 'Let me take the speck out of your eye,' when all the time there is a plank in your own eye? You hypocrite, first take the plank out of your own eye, and then you will see clearly to remove the speck from your brother's eye."

Matthew 7: 1-5

The NIV Life Application Bible commentary says: "Jesus' statement, "Do not judge," is against the kind of hypocritical, judgmental attitude that tears others down in order to build oneself up. It is not a blanket statement against all critical thinking, but <u>a call to be discerning rather than negative</u>. Jesus said to expose false teachers (Matthew 7:15-23), and Paul taught that we should exercise church discipline (I Corinthians 5:1-2) and trust God to be the final judge (I Corinthians 4:3-5)."

With all that said, we need to try to not judge others as much as possible because we are all *unique* children of God. For women, this usually comes in the form of comparison and we all do it. We compare ourselves to each other and compare our kids to others' kids and our husbands to others' husbands. We compare our appearances with the appearances of others. We need to remember: I Samuel 16:7 But the Lord said to Samuel, "Do not consider his appearance or height, for I have rejected him. The Lord does not look at the things man looks at. Man looks at the outward appearance, *but the Lord looks at the heart.*"

We are all uniquely made and instead of trying to make us all into cookie cutter copies, we need to respect our differences and learn from them. We *all* have strengths and weaknesses. *Beauty fades and riches can be lost, but we forget to keep that perspective when we begin the comparing game. We have to look past the outside appearances and see people for who they really are.* Don't make assumptions based on the little you see of another's outside appearance or circumstances. It seems like every time I have judged someone, God allowed similar circumstances into my life in order to humble me and cause me to repent for judging them. *God loves to help His kids to grow to maturity in Him. ;-)*

Often times, we get jealous of someone else's strength that is our weakness or we judge them because we don't understand them. There is a better way to handle our differences. *If we choose to, we can glean from others' strengths in order to grow in the weak areas of our own lives. Or we can choose to respect about them what we don't understand.* An example from my life is my friend Anna. She has incredible people skills and would talk to strangers all the time. I was on the road of growing out of my shy nature when God put her into my life. I was amazed at how easily she spoke to strangers in any setting. I wanted to be able to do that too. What kept me from speaking to strangers was my fear of rejection. So I watched how people responded to her. Not once did anyone bite her head off for beginning a conversation with them which destroyed my theory that rejection was eminent. After watching her and praying for God's help to grow in this area, I began to step out in faith and start up conversations with strangers in the supermarket or at church...*and everyone was nice.* The truth I learned is that everyone is waiting for the other person to reach out in friendliness. This is because our culture has trained us to believe that there are invisible walls of privacy between people in elevators and in check out lines etc. So, instead of judging Anna and thinking she was bold and inconsiderate of the invisible walls, I chose to glean from her strength and it has paid off huge in my life.

We all struggle with judging strangers out in public either on the roads or in stores. But we don't think about why they may be displaying such odd behaviors. They may have just been given bad news or have health issues they are dealing with. Gary has had some major medical issues recently including three mini-strokes. The third stroke caused him to loose peripheral vision in his right eye which caused his equilibrium and bearings to be off while he was healing. He would run into things while pushing a cart at the grocery store or be extremely cautious with each step he took. When we see people out in public, it is easy to judge them because we assume they are healthy and functioning in a normal capacity. But we really don't know if their odd behavior is due to serious health issues or depression or bad news they just received. We should not judge others since we don't know what issues they may be walking.

We've all been on the other side of the coin as well when people have judged us, but you shouldn't worry about what others think. We need to worry about what God thinks and live according to how He teaches us to live through the Bible. We must live our lives based on God's standards of right and wrong rather than conform to the world's standards or others' expectations of us. You will never be able to please all of the people all of the time because people are too complicated for that. You can't even please many people some of the time. Everyone has different opinions anyway and often their opinions change based on who they are with. So don't focus on pleasing people. *Focus on pleasing God and you will have less heartache overall.* In the end…we will stand before God to be judged; not people!

> "To fear the Lord is to hate evil; I hate pride and arrogance, evil behavior and perverse speech."
>
> Proverbs 8:13

The main reason why we slip into judging others is the root sin of pride. *Pride makes us think that we are better than others and that we are right!* The Bible says that God hates pride. He is opposed to the proud and haughty in every generation. Instead, He is drawn to those who are humble and meek both spiritually and physically. They will be rewarded because they trust in God. Self-reliance and prideful arrogance should have no place among God's people or in His kingdom. Your life belongs to Jesus! Be His living sacrifice!

> JUDGING HURTS EVERYONE! WE NEED TO LET GOD BE THE JUDGE! GLEAN FROM OTHERS RATHER THAN JUDGING THEM!

WE ARE ALL GIFTED!

"The body is a unit, though it is made up of many parts; and though all its parts are many, they form one body. So it is with Christ. For we were all baptized by one Spirit into one body— whether Jews or Greeks, slave or free— and we were all given the one Spirit to drink. Now the body is not made up of one part but of many. If the foot should say, "Because I am not a hand, I do not belong to the body," it would not for that reason cease to be part of the body. And if the ear should say, "Because I am not an eye, I do not belong to the body," it would not for that reason cease to be part of the body. If the whole body were an eye, where would the sense of hearing be? If the whole body were an ear, where would the sense of smell be? But in fact God has arranged the parts in the body, every one of them, just as he wanted them to be. If they were all one part, where would the body be? As it is, there are many parts, but one body. The eye cannot say to the hand, "I don't need you!" And the head cannot say to the feet, "I don't need you!" On the contrary, those parts of the body that seem to be weaker are indispensable, and the parts that we think are less honorable we treat with special honor. And the parts that are not presentable are treated with special modesty, while our presentable parts need no special treatment. But God has combined the members of the body and has given greater honor to the parts that lacked it, so that there should be no division in the body, but that its parts should have equal concern for each other. If one part suffers, every part suffers with it; if one part is honored, every part rejoices with it. Now you are the body of Christ, and each one of you is a part of it."

I Corinthians 12:12- 27

This passage of Scripture is something we all need to be reminded of frequently. We, as individuals, do not make a whole body. It is only as we combine all of our talents, giftings and personalities that God has given to each one of us, will we begin to make a whole body. This can be seen the easiest in the immediate family and in the church family. *We all need each other. None of us are designed to do it all alone.* We all have our part to play within our family and in our church family. Within our personal family, Gary and I have established each of our roles based on our talents, strengths and abilities, yet our roles have changed over the years based on our personal growth and what needed to be accomplished in each season of life. Our kid's roles are always changing as they mature, but the parts that they play are just as valuable. As time goes on, we all change and our roles will fluctuate accordingly. We need to become kingdom-minded and comfortable enough to operate in our own abilities within both of these arenas. The Kingdom of God is most efficient when we value everyone and when we each play our part in the body of Christ with gusto and generosity. We must respect and value the role each one of us plays and allow the changes that time brings to happen smoothly and without conflict.

Let's use the military as an example. There are different divisions of the military: Navy, Army, Marines and Air Force. Within each of those divisions they continue to break down their authority structure and duties. They all need each other to effectively defend our country. The cook is as important as the general because the soldiers have to eat. In God's eyes we all play our part and the pastor is not of higher value to Him than the janitor. As long as we are using our talents, and personalities to the best of our ability and for His glory, then God is pleased. James 2:26 "As the body without the spirit is dead, so faith without deeds is dead."

> BE ALL THAT GOD DESIGNED YOU TO BE IN HIS KINGDOM AND HE WILL BE GLORIFIED! WE ARE ALL SERVANTS OF THE LORD!

CONTENTMENT & THANKFULNESS

"I am not saying this because I am in need, for I have learned to be content whatever the circumstances. I know what it is to be in need, and I know what it is to have plenty. I have learned the secret of being content in any and every situation, whether well fed or hungry, whether living in plenty or in want. I can do everything through him who gives me strength."

Philippians 4:11-13

"Do not store up for your selves' treasures on earth, where moth and rust destroy, and where thieves break in and steal. But store up for your selves treasures in heaven, where moth and rust do not destroy, and where thieves do not break in and steal. For where your treasure is, there your heart will be also."

Matthew 6:19-21

We live in a culture that teaches us to be discontent and ungrateful for what we have. Commercials and sales pitches are designed to stir up the desire in our hearts to have what we don't have, in order to be something we don't need to be, so we can impress people we don't even know. This battleground is one we face *daily*. We have to be aware of this tactic of Satan or we will lose our joy. Inner joy comes from the *choice* to be content and thankful. We have to make a conscious effort to see the cup as half full instead of half empty. We have to stop and count our blessings and see how they out-weigh the difficulties or the lack in our lives. I Thessalonians 5:16-18 "Be joyful always; pray continually; give thanks in all circumstances, for this is God's will for you in Christ Jesus." We have to look at the positive traits of our family and friends and focus on them rather than focus on their negative traits. We still need to train the negative traits out of our kids and lovingly walk our husbands and ourselves out of our negative traits, but those negative traits cannot be our focal point. If all we focus on is our weaknesses, then we lose sight of how wonderful our strengths are.

We previously discussed the negative consequences of the comparison game. Only in the following way can we use the comparison game. We will always meet other people whose life circumstances are harder than ours. This is a gift from God to remind us that our circumstances aren't as bad as we think they are. These insights help us to re-focus our wrong thinking. God has chosen different kinds of crosses for each one of us to bear and each cross is specifically designed with His personal knowledge of what each one of us can handle. Trust Him that He is in control of the tools He is using to shape you more into His image.

Being thankful is a choice. As we begin to grumble about our circumstances we need to stop, ask for God's forgiveness, and ask Him to change our hearts to begin to trust Him and rest in His sovereignty in our lives. We must also remember to send Him "thank you prayers" when He has answered our prayers. Just like we love to be thanked when we meet the needs of our loved ones, God loves to be thanked when He meets our needs. We need to thank Him when we see how He has protected us from harmful circumstances. I know that we have had many "close calls" while driving in the car and we knew God was protecting us. We always took the time to thank Him afterwards.

> "But godliness with contentment is great gain. For we brought nothing into the world, and we can take nothing out of it."
>
> I Timothy 6:6-7

We need to thank Him for all that we have and maintain a heart of gratitude daily. We are all so blessed with our families, homes, vehicles, and day-to-day provision. Remind yourself to not take anything for granted. Even if we are living in a shack, we must be thankful for a roof over our heads. This is another kingdom principle that we must be thankful for what little we have and steward it well before God will bless us with more. God is so good to us and always faithful!

We should also thank Him in advance for the things we are praying about or waiting for. It's like saying thank you to your husband for picking up the kids for you later on today. God loves to be thanked before things happen as well.

Another way to show our gratitude to God is to sing worship songs to Him at any available opportunity.

Psalm 92:1-2 "It is good to praise the Lord and make music to your name, O Most High, to proclaim your love in the morning and your faithfulness at night…" He will meet you there in an incredible way. He loves to interact with us in those personal moments. Don't miss out on these special aspects of your relationship with God.

> I PRAISE YOU AND THANK YOU,
> LORD, FOR WHO YOU ARE TO ME
> AND FOR EVERYTHING YOU HAVE
> BLESSED ME WITH!

BE A GOOD LISTENER! TAME YOUR TONGUE!

People don't care about how much you know until they know how much you care!

The Lord has taught me that an incredible tool I can use for Him is to be a good listener. This means I need to talk less and listen more. As I listen I will ask questions for clarification of information as I focus on them. I have to maintain eye contact and my body language needs to stay engaged in the conversation as well. When I listen intently, the person begins to feel safe because many people today are more interested in them selves or are too busy on their cell phones to listen to others' struggles. I have found that the more I listen…I am better able to gather insight into the bigger picture in order to receive wisdom from the Holy Spirit on how to encourage them. There are also times when people just need a place to vent their pent-up feelings and struggles, and just being heard and receiving a hug helps them to release what is bottled up inside. This investment of my time is showing the love of Jesus to others and being 'Jesus with skin on.'

(Note: This will also help you know how to pray more specifically for them. If someone confides in you, be sure to keep whatever private matters they shared to yourself.)

We are inundated with people's words all day long through the media and in our homes. But how good are we at listening when our loved ones talk. *Listening is a skill to be learned!* God gave us two ears and one mouth so we should listen twice as much as we speak. People spend up to $150 an hour to go to therapists in order to have some one listen to them when they talk. This is partly because our culture today talks more than it listens. We all want to be heard and understood. We all want to be listened to by a person who is a safe place and who will listen intently to the cries of our hearts. Well, if we all want it and no one is giving it, then maybe we should all work on becoming sincere listeners.

Every one of us is hurting at some level! Each one of us has broken areas in our lives that we long for someone to walk with us through. *God did not design us to do life alone.* He created us to walk through the hardships of our lives together.

> "If anyone considers himself religious, and yet does not keep a tight rein on his tongue, he deceives himself and his religion is worthless."
>
> James 1:26

> "Likewise the tongue is a small part of the body, but it makes great boasts. Consider what a great forest is set on fire by a small spark. The tongue also is a fire, a world of evil among the parts of the body. It corrupts the whole person, sets the whole course of his life on fire, and is itself set on fire by hell. All kinds of animals, birds, reptiles, and creatures of the sea are being tamed

by man, but no man can tame the tongue. It is a restless evil, full of deadly poison."

James 3:5-8

There is power in our words! If God "spoke" everything into existence, and we are made in His image, then we need to think about what our words may be speaking into existence!

We all know how powerful our words can be whether we are saying them or receiving them. We must work hard to make sure that we are lifting others up rather than tearing them down. No one wants to be verbally torn down. When we tear others down with our words we usually feel convicted afterwards. We must stop ourselves from speaking negative things over our children's lives as well, because we are speaking those things into existence. An example is to say I am so stupid or calling another person stupid. We are then professing stupidity over who ever it is. Likewise, we must be purposeful about speaking positive things over their lives; therefore speaking those things into existence. An example is we can speak prophetically over ourselves and those we love such as I am an overcomer through Jesus Christ. Scripture is full of verses we can uses as prophetic prayers over our life or the lives of our loved ones. Just a few examples are:

"God has not give me a spirit of fear, but one of power, love and a sound mind."

II Timothy 1:7

"I take every thought captive unto the obedience of Jesus Christ, casting down every imagination, and every high and lofty thing that exalts itself against the knowledge of God."

II Corinthians 10:5

"I am dead to sin but alive to God."

Romans 6:11

When we are verbally berated, we should try to not respond and just keep our mouth shut and turn the other cheek. This is easier said than done but as we continue to grow in our relationship with Jesus, He helps us to act like Him and control what we say and how we respond. There have been many times when I wanted to respond to ugly words directed at me, but I kept my mouth shut because I was too angry to respond with kindness. Then afterwards, as I mulled it all over in my mind, I thought of all the things I could have said that would have put them straight and spoke what was on my mind. The truth is, after I had cooled down, I was glad that my words could not be used against me because I had not spoken them. Then I only had to fix my heart with the Lord instead of having to apologize to the person for things I had said. Proverbs 17:26-27 "A man of knowledge uses words with restraint, and a man of understanding is even-tempered. Even a fool is thought wise if he keeps silent, and discerning if he holds his tongue." As we continue to mature in the Lord, we practice learning how to control our thoughts as well as control our words. Proverbs 29:11 "A fool gives full vent to his anger, but a wise man keeps himself under control."

If we need to speak the truth to someone, we need to speak it in love. Proverbs 24:26 "An honest answer is like a kiss on the lips." Sometimes God uses a close friend or loved one to speak a truth that we need to hear and we need to have the grace to receive it. Proverbs 27:5-6a "Better is open rebuke than hidden love. Wounds from a friend can be trusted." Proverbs 27:17 says: "As iron sharpens iron, so one man sharpens another."

Proverbs 29:23 "A man's pride brings him low, but a man of lowly spirit gains honor." Pride causes us to say and do so many ungodly things. It can even cause us to tell lies or exaggerate the truth to make ourselves look good to someone else. Instead, we need to be humble about who we are before God and not try to puff ourselves up with flattering words. Proverbs 27:2 "Let another praise you, and not your own mouth; someone else, and not your own lips."

I Timothy 6:20b-21a "Turn away from godless chatter and the opposing ideas of what is falsely called knowledge, which some have professed and in so doing have wandered from the faith." Godless chatter is so common today and it definitely distracts us from the truth. We have to be so careful in this area because it is somewhat addicting, especially for us women. Facebook is an easy avenue for us to express godless chatter, opposing ideas, and be influenced by false knowledge, so be aware and cautious.

As fellow Christians, we will have different doctrinal views on many topics. The age old saying goes: *We must find unity in the essentials, liberty in the non-essentials, and love above all things.* We need to work harder at focusing on the foundational truths of Christianity while giving grace in the non-essentials where there is more disagreement. The church as a whole needs to work on taming its tongue. We must unify as we face the end times. *We are on the same team!*

> "Not that I have already obtained all this, or have already been made perfect, but I press on to take hold of that for which Christ Jesus took hold of me. Brothers, I do not consider myself yet to have taken hold of it. But one thing I do: Forgetting what is behind and straining toward what is ahead, I press on toward the goal to win the prize for which God has called me heavenward in Christ Jesus. All of us who are mature should take such a view of things. And if on some point you think differently, that too God will make clear to you. Only let us live up to what we have already attained."
>
> Philippians 3:12-16

HELP ME, LORD, TO TAME MY TONGUE AND BE A GOOD LISTENER!

ATTITUDE

If you have a good attitude, you will get the task done quickly and efficiently. If you maintain a bad attitude, the task will become a mountain that you will never climb.

Attitude is 90% of a task and the work you put into it is only 10%. This is pivotal to our success at everything in life. How we view our circumstances and responsibilities determines how successful and efficient we will be at completing them. This is something I share with our kids regarding their school work. Whenever they give in to having an attitude, it is like their minds shut off while we are doing school and no matter what I try to teach them it does not compute. I send them to their room to adjust their attitude so I don't waste my energy trying to teach them something that they are not in the right frame of mind to receive. We as people are the same way. If we have an attitude about something, it becomes the hardest thing we have ever done. When we feel like we are being *forced* to complete a task and have an attitude, it is like running into a brick wall.

When we as individuals get like this, we need to get away from people and get alone with God. We need to pray to Him and ask Him to change our attitude and correct our wrong thinking. We have to allow the Holy Spirit to help us get the courage to face that mountain which is usually motivated by fear, feeling overwhelmed, or a lack of desire to complete the necessary task. Only as we face these obstacles head on and change our attitude about them can we climb the huge mountain and gain *victory*.

> "If anyone serves, he should do it with the strength God provides, so that in all things God may be praised through Jesus Christ. To him be the glory and the power for ever and ever. Amen."
>
> I Peter 4:11b

Let's use an example of cleaning the house. We have no desire to do it and are overwhelmed by it. So, we first realize that we have an attitude about doing it. We stop and ask God to help us overcome our attitude and face the overwhelming task. Then we change how we view the task. I choose to be thankful that we have food to eat to dirty the dishes that I now get to wash. I choose to be thankful that I can wash the clothes God has blessed me with in a washer and dryer and not have to wash them by hand and hang them on a clothes line like my ancestors did. I choose to thank God for my tile and carpet and machines to clean them with since many homes in the third world only have dirt for their floors. I thank God for my indoor plumbing and hot water that I get to clean with and enjoy using daily because many homes in the third world have no hot water and use an outhouse as a restroom. *Perspective is everything!* We are *so blessed* and we don't even realize it. We take our luxuries for granted. My experience in the Philippines has had a lasting imprint on my view of all the beautiful amenities that we have in America and in the world. Don't take for granted how much easier it is to maintain a household today compared to the men and women who developed our country through hard, manual work. I Corinthians 10:31 "So whether you eat or drink or whatever you do, do it all for the glory of God." Most of our time is spent maintaining the daily, boring, and mundane responsibilities of life. This is actually where we show our true Christian walk—by doing it all for His glory! It is vital that we grasp the concept that we are really doing every task as unto the Lord. Do everything with love and excellence in honor of your Creator. *God is watching and He will reward you for your service done with the right heart attitude.*

Clutter makes us feel overwhelmed. Sometimes our homes are not dirty as much as they are cluttered. Work hard to keep things picked up and in their place to help your home feel more under control. Organization makes us feel secure and clutter makes us feel scatter-brained.

How do you eat an elephant? The answer is: "One bite at a time." If the task before you is overwhelming, then start by only biting off one bite of the huge task at a time. Then another bite and so on until the task is done. I live by the rule of: Get your work done and then you can play. This is what is expected of my kids too. For me, I need to get my responsibilities done and then I can do the things I really want to do.

If you struggle with keeping your house clean and organized and need a resource to help you learn how to grow in this area, I suggest reading some books by Emilie Barnes: *The Quick Fix Home Organizer: Making*

Your Home Beautiful and Your Life Clutter Free and/or
101 Ways to Clean Out the Clutter

> WHENEVER YOU ARE STRUGGLING WITH AN ATTITUDE...ASK THE HOLY SPIRIT TO HELP YOU TO CHANGE IT...HE LOVES TO HELP US BECOME AN OVERCOMER!

RESPECT AND HONOR

"Now we ask you, brothers, to respect those who work hard among you, who are over you in the Lord and who admonish you. Hold them in the highest regard in love because of their work. Live in peace with each other."

I Thessalonians 5:12-13

Most of us only honor others for what they do or show them respect for the position of authority that they hold. God wants us to honor and respect everyone! We all expect others to show us respect/honor, but we often don't think we should have to give respect/honor to others unless it is merited. This is a kingdom principle that in order to receive it, we have to first give it. Just the fact that they are a human being created in the image of God is deserving of respect and honor. It is only as we give respect/honor to our parents, husbands, children, bosses and friends we will then in return receive it. Of course we will run into those individuals who will not reciprocate it, but they are probably operating out of their brokenness. God wants us to honor one another. He commands us to honor one another above ourselves. If we don't receive what our actions deserve on this earth, then we will receive our reward with the Lord in heaven. All God asks us to do is obey His command to honor and respect others above ourselves.

Exodus 20:12 "Honor your father and your mother, so that you may live long in the land the Lord your God is giving you." None of us have perfect parents. Once we become parents we find that we aren't perfect parents either. As we enter into parenthood we begin to see how hard and long-term parenting really is. This realization should leave us with more of a grace-filled understanding for our parents as we acknowledge the struggles they also had while raising us. Life is hard for everyone. Marriage and parenting are hard for everyone.

It also helps us to honor our parents if we look at how they were raised. The issues they faced as children shaped them positively and negatively as well. When we have been wronged by our parents we usually make an "inner vow" to go to the other extreme in that area or we take on that same "iniquity" or learned behavior. An example of an "inner vow" is when a person was raised by a very strict disciplinarian and hated it, so he now has very little discipline with his children. We need to not fluctuate between the extremes, but instead find a healthy balance in the middle of the two parenting philosophies. An example of the same learned behavior is an abusive alcoholic. The child hates being abused, but often grows up to follow the same behavior. This is a generational curse that needs to be broken through the power of Jesus. He is the one who can set us free from this kind of bondage. As we look at the life factors that shaped *our* parents, we can have more grace for them and give them the honor they deserve for being our parents.

By honoring our parents we are opening up the doors for God to give us long life. We all have issues and disagreements with our parents, but we can still show them honor and respect in what we say to them and in how we say it. We can show the love of Jesus to them in multiple ways. We can take the time to maintain a relationship with them as a way of thanking them for all they did for us as we were children in their care. We must also say the words, "Thank you!" to them for all they did for us over the years. For those of you who were abused or abandoned by your parents, you can honor them by offering forgiveness and trying to offer them Jesus. If they still refuse your love or God's love…just keep praying for them.

> "Be devoted to one another in brotherly love. Honor one another above yourselves. Never be lacking in zeal, but keep your spiritual fervor, serving the Lord."
>
> Romans 12:10-11

The number one need of a man is to receive honor. Wives, this responsibility falls heavily onto us. We have to show our husbands honor/respect and we have to teach our children to honor/respect their father. Satan has used our current culture to strip men of their manhood while it encourages men to be selfish and irresponsible. Because of this attack on men I assume that there are many of your husbands who don't deserve honor and respect. But if you give them honor in whatever areas you see him succeeding in, God will honor your obedience. We can also show honor to our husbands by keeping our mouth shut from our criticism. Our words have a strong negative affect on our man. We should thank our husbands for the daily things in life that he does do faithfully like going to work or paying the bills etc. When we say, "Thank you, honey, for all you do…I sure appreciate you!" it goes a long way to making him feel honored.

We have to show honor and respect to our kids as we discipline them. The power of life and death are in the tongue. Often how and what we say to our kids is not thought through and does damage to their self-esteem. We've all watched the faces of our kids fall after we have verbally cut them down. There is just as much power in our words when we say things that lift them up. Their faces light up with pride for making Mom proud. We all have to work hard at disciplining our kids with the respect and honor in our words, tone of voice, and body language. Whenever it is possible, pull your child aside and discipline them privately to help them keep their dignity.

Lastly, we have to give honor and respect to those in authority over us. Our bosses and our government are ordered by God. Romans 13: 1-2 "Let every soul be subject to the governing authorities. For there is no authority except from God, and the authorities that exist are appointed by God. Therefore whoever resists the authority resists the ordinance of God, and those who resist will bring judgment on themselves." This is a kingdom principle that doesn't seem to make sense when those in authority over us are unjust or ungodly. Sometimes God allows these kinds of people to stay in leadership for a time, in order to serve other purposes He may have. *God's sovereignty is trustworthy.* He uses difficult authorities in our lives to cause us to cling to Him for help and strengthen us during the adversity. A great resource for learning more about understanding honor is a book by John Bevere: *Honor's Reward.* Check it out at www.messengerinternational.org. You'll be blessed! Proverbs 22:4 "Humility and the fear of the Lord bring wealth and honor and life."

> TEST GOD AS YOU CHOOSE TO OBEY HIM BY HONORING EVERYONE IN YOUR LIFE. SEE HOW HE USES IT TO EITHER GROW YOU OR CHANGE THEM...OR BOTH!

COMMUNICATION IN MARRIAGE

> "Don't have anything to do with foolish and stupid arguments, because you know they produce quarrels. And the Lord's servant must not quarrel; instead, he must be kind to everyone, able to teach, not resentful."
>
> 2 Timothy 2:23-24

Communication is done through words we say, the tone in our voice, body language, and things we do. We need to be aware of how we are communicating in all these ways. We want to show our love and the love of Jesus to those around us.

We all need to work hard at communicating more effectively. How well we communicate really impacts our marriage relationship. We go into marriage with the idea that if we have found the perfect man, then we won't have to work as hard as we did while we were courting him. Wrong! We need to keep courting our mate after we say "I do." Unfortunately, we often get lazy in the area of communication but when we do, everything begins to unravel. We are blessed today with cell phones (texting), email, face book etc. which makes it easier to stay on the same page with our spouse. In addition to giving one another information about ourselves or the kids, we need to communicate our love frequently. We need to say, "I love you!" We need to touch each other, hug each other, joke around and kiss often. Keep flirting with and dating your husband! We must keep working on our relationship until we go home to be with Jesus. Only as we work hard at this can we keep our marriage relationship strong.

As women we need to remember to be sensitive to our husband's time. When he is stressed out or in a time crunch, we shouldn't share all the little details with him that we are anxious to tell. Just give him the main points and save the details for another opportunity when time isn't a factor and he is more relaxed. We need to learn to condense our information and still be an effective communicator.

You have heard people say marriage should be a 50/50% give and take. That is not what the Bible teaches. Gary and I have chosen to view marriage as a 100/100% give and take. If I am working hard to make sure all of his needs are met and he is working hard to make sure all of my needs are met, then, we have very little to fight about.

> "Jesus knew their thoughts and said to them: "Any kingdom divided against itself will be ruined, and a house divided against itself will fall."
>
> Luke 11:17

As we become parents, we need to work as a team against the kids and the only way to do this is through effective communication. If either parent is missing vital information…the kids *will* take advantage of it. They are designed to always test the boundaries. They want to push on those boundaries to find out if they are strong and secure. As they find the boundaries to be secure, they will give in to your leadership and 'rest' in knowing that they are safe under your care. (They will still test those boundaries at various times through out their entire life under your roof.) You and your husband are a team and your kids are a team. We take turns playing offense and defense but *whose side of the team you are on needs to be firmly set.* We were once told that: us against one child is two on one defense. After the second child it becomes man to man defense. Then when the third child or more come along, it becomes zone defense. Always work as a team against them and be a united front. United we stand, but divided we fall. Take the time to talk through the issues with your spouse in a private room and then stand firm on the decisions the two of you make. If you disagree with your spouse while around the children, ask to speak to him/her privately to discuss it so the kids can't use that disagreement against you. At times it is easy to slip into the habit of siding with the kids against our husband since we are usually the one who are in tune with meeting all their needs. But in the end, it divides you against your husband. We may also feel like the kids will never be gone, but the day will come when they will leave and move on with their lives. None of us want to end up with a bad case of 'empty nest syndrome.' This happens when we no longer have a relationship with our husband because everything about our relationship revolved around the children. This is why many couples divorce after their kids move out. Instead, our goal is to still be close to our husband when the kids move out because all that will be left is the two of us: the husband/wife team. It began with just the two of you (unless you are a blended family), and God-willing it will end with the two of you as well.

It is more beneficial for both spouses to discuss all the financial decisions in your marriage and know where the family money is being spent. God gifted each of you with different viewpoints toward money and if you will glean from each viewpoint, you will make much wiser financial decisions.

We also need to teach good communication skills to our kids and this is a hard, yet rewarding process. Actually, this has been a *daily* area of training in our home. The way our kids talk to one another or the way they respond to me or Gary is always on our radar. They have to learn how to use self-control with their words, how to control the tone in their voices, and how to control their anger too. God wants us to teach them these skills while they are in our care. Even their outward appearance, body odor, or controlling the gum in their mouths needs to be parented so others around them do not have to deal with their childhood or puberty issues. This is our opportunity to give them the necessary tools of communication they each need to thrive in society as adults.

Always tell the truth to the people in your life. "You shall not give false testimony against your neighbor." Exodus 20:16 God is honored when we obey Him and telling the truth is one of His commandments. If we need to tell the difficult truth to someone in our life, try to say the truth with tons of love and a kind, loving tone and body language. We have to teach this to our children too. We get plenty of opportunities to teach this to them as they interact with their siblings.

Many of you may feel like this is all good and true information, but my husband won't do his part. Marriage is under attack today and Satan's many lies have infiltrated our culture and are still working to destroy our marriage relationships. Satan's game plan is to destroy the marriage which then destroys the kids and then destroys society. Gary and I are using an incredible marriage series that addresses *all* of those issues. Each time we take people through it we see breakthrough and victory in their marriages. It is "Marriage on the Rock" by Pastor Jimmy Evans. Go to www.marriagetoday.org to find out how to purchase it. This series also helps great marriages become even greater. Pastor Jimmy also has many other incredible series available as well that will bless and enhance your marriage.

If you are a single mother, then press in to Jesus who will be your husband. Also make sure you have a church and good friends as your support group. Use them as your sounding board on the difficult issues you face as you parent those kids alone.

COMMUNICATION IS HARD
AND A TON OF WORK...
BUT THE FRUIT OF IT
IS WELL WORTH IT!

BE AN ENCOURAGER!

WALK AS A "WOUNDED-HEALER!" THE WOUNDS IN OUR LIVES, AFTER THEY ARE HEALED, LEAVE SCARS THAT ALLOW US TO MINISTER TO OTHERS WITH A HEART FULL OF COMPASSION AND GRACE.

Life is hard no matter who you are. Life always brings us difficult times and twists and turns that leave us confused and hurting. As we realize that all of us experience hard times in life, then we can begin to make ourselves available to encourage others when they are hurting. Encouragement is not that difficult if you allow the Holy Spirit to lead you. It can be as simple as a smile or a loving touch. Or it can be many words of encouragement along with a hug and crying with them. We can make a meal or send a card or care for someone's child. We can send a gift or clean their house or just be a good listener. We can even ask the Holy Spirit to give us a Scripture passage, to send in a text or e-mail that would be a blessing to them or pray for/with them. You can really let your creative juices flow when it comes to ways to be an encourager. Whatever it is, people are blessed when others take the time to bless them. Keep in mind, that God sees our actions and will reward us in His own way. Many times as we step out in faith and encourage others, God will then bring people to encourage us when we need it as well.

We already talked about how we are all gifted in different ways. Encouragement is one of the gifts that God has given to me. All of the above suggestions are so much fun to do. When Gary was working at the large church in California, the Holy Spirit showed me how tired and overwhelmed all of the staff was. The church was growing so fast and so were their work loads with no end in sight. The Holy Spirit gave me the idea of blessing each of them with a gift or candy of some kind and a note of encouragement from the Scripture or a quote from one of my devotionals each month. It was supposed to be a secret. Each month I would prepare something different and Gary and I would sneak in to the church mail room and fill all forty-five of their boxes with this surprise. I signed it each time with a smiley face. I became known as "smiley face" although no one knew who it was. Since Gary worked there, he was able to watch and hear their reactions. They were all encouraged by the notes and had something to look forward to each month that didn't require something from them. It became fun for them to try to figure out who "smiley face" was. They began accusing one another to try to see who the culprit was. We succeeded in encouraging them for a year until the time came when God moved us here to Texas. They were all so shocked to find out it was us and were so blessed by everything we had done. We were blessed doing it and had a blast being undercover secret agents of encouragement.

View being an encourager as a privilege. You can be God's servant on special assignment sent to another one of 'His kids.' There is such a deep joy when you get to watch someone who is discouraged have their spirits lifted as you touch their life. Enjoy this special gift from God of helping to lift others out of the muck and mire through encouragement.

> "Therefore encourage one another and build each other up, just as in fact you are doing. Now we ask you, brothers, to respect those who work hard among you, who are over you in the Lord and who admonish you. Hold them in the highest regard in love because of their work. Live in peace with each other. And we urge you, brothers, warn those who are idle, encourage the timid help the weak, be patient with everyone. Make sure that nobody pays back wrong for wrong, but always try to be kind to each other and to everyone else."
>
> I Thessalonians 5:11-15

BECOME THE TOOL GOD USES TO TOUCH OTHERS' LIVES!

GOD WILL PROVIDE!

> "So do not fear, for I am with you; do not be dismayed, for I am your God. I will strengthen you and help you; I will up hold you with my righteous right hand."
>
> Isaiah 41:10

Gary and I got pregnant with our first child on our honeymoon. At the time, Gary worked at a Christian school teaching and coaching and we did not have any health insurance. But due to our low income, we were able to go to the doctor through the help of state aid. Our desire was for me to be a stay-at-home mom so I never went to work since it would be hard to find a job that would hire a pregnant woman who would soon quit. Gary's salary that year was $17,600 so we were scraping by. Toward the end of that year the Christian school he worked at met with their teachers to tell them that they would not be receiving anymore paychecks because the school was in trouble and the teachers just needed to "live by faith." Tell that to our landlord! Through a friend the Lord provided a job at the Coca Cola warehouse for Gary and he worked there through the summer. Next, God provided a better job for the following school year at another Christian school that offered incredible insurance. Believe it or not, we had our first child at Kaiser Permanente hospital in Fontana, California. Our insurance began on September 1st and she was born on September 21st.

I was never able to meet with a doctor until her birth and the whole birth was covered by the insurance. Isn't God amazing! Gary worked for one year at this school, but private education doesn't pay very well so…

God orchestrated circumstances where Gary got a job as an athletic trainer and adult education teacher at Rialto High School which was a brand new school opening up that next year. They also offered Kaiser Insurance so were able to have our remaining three children there for free during the twelve years he worked at Rialto High. Glory to God! Gary's hours and wages continued to increase over the years as our family grew in size. God provided the increase each time we needed it.

We chose for me to home school our kids in order to have more time to invest in their character training and to avoid many of the negative influences of the public school system in California. We always struggled financially to make ends meet due to this decision. We had some college debt when we first married that we added to here and there when our one car needed repairs because there was no extra money for surprise expenses. About five years into our marriage, Gary incurred a back injury as the volunteer youth pastor while we were at youth camp. It was during game time when the referee called the youth pastors to come and play the game of "steal the bacon." It was a contest to pull a large inner tube across a line to win. The other youth pastor decided to sweep Gary's feet to win and Gary landed straight on his tail bone and ruptured two of his discs in the vertebrae of his lower back. The church we were serving at had workman's comp insurance that happened to cover volunteer workers. That injury and settlement was God's financial provision for our debt at that time. We were so excited to see Him work through those difficult circumstances.

> "Honor the Lord with your wealth, with the first fruits of all your crops; then your barns will be filled to overflowing, and your vats will brim over with new wine."
>
> Proverbs 3:9-10

The Bible teaches that we should give from our first fruits, but we need to first understand that we don't actually own anything. *It all belongs to God!* Our bodies, health, jobs, mates, children and physical assets all belong to God. We can only care for them because God continues to bless us with the health to maintain our livelihoods and wisdom to make wise decisions. *The sooner we realize that we are nothing without God, the more we will value all that He has blessed us with. As we value all that He has blessed us with, then we will treat it as valuable. When we treat everything with value, then God chooses to bless us with more because we become a trustworthy steward who will not waste or cheapen what God has given.*

We also need to understand that God will only give us what we can handle, no more, no less. *We are stewards of all that He gives us and it is our responsibility to use His blessings for His glory.* One day we will all stand before Him and have to give account for every thing and every person He placed in our lives. Did we wisely steward all the physical and financial blessings God gave us? Did we help our mate and children to blossom and grow into healthy children of our King of Kings? I am not saying that if your child chooses to rebel against God as an adult that you should live under condemnation. They are then accountable to God for the choices that they make. You are accountable for the things you did while they were in your care. Yet, in all of the areas where we failed the ones who were in our care, we can still ask God for His forgiveness and receive it. It is covered under the blood of Christ. None of us are perfect, but we must always keep growing to become more like Jesus in every area including how we manage all that God has entrusted to our care.

As we choose to make God a priority in our finances, He provides in many ways. His provision comes through money, good health, good health insurance, appliances that don't break, protection from lawsuits, sale items, gifts from others, etc. Be sure you look at all the ways God is providing for you and thank and praise Him for it.

We have to fight the tendencies toward materialism that we see in all aspects of our world. Things go out of style every year and it is costly to try to always keep up with the Jones. Billy Graham once said: "I've never seen a hearse pulling a U-haul truck."

> YOU CAN'T TAKE IT WITH YOU,
> BUT YOU CAN SEND IT ON AHEAD!

OPPOSITE SEX GUIDELINES AND INTIMACY WITH YOUR HUSBAND

"But since there is so much immorality, each man should have his own wife, and each woman her own husband. The husband should fulfill his marital duty to his wife, and likewise the wife to her husband. In the same way, the husband's body does not belong to him alone but also to his wife. Do not deprive each other except by mutual consent and for a time, so that you may devote yourselves to prayer. Then come together again so that Satan will not tempt you because of your lack of self-control."

I Corinthians 7:2-5

"Marriage should be honored by all, and the marriage bed kept pure, for God will judge the adulterer and all the sexually immoral."

Hebrews 13:4

One of the naïve things I thought as a young woman entering marriage was that other men would view me as off-limits and no longer look at me with interest or flirt with me anymore. I don't know why I thought that except it was the innocence of my youth. As you probably know, this is not true. Even married Christian men who are discontent in their marriages will test us to see if we respond to their advances. We first have to decide in our hearts to obey God's Biblical plan to stay faithful to our husbands and then ask God to help us to succeed. We also need to use some practical methods to help us along the way. When you began flirting with your future husband, you probably began by flirting through eye contact. Likewise, this is how most men begin flirting with you when you are married. With this understanding, we need to be careful with whom we make direct eye contact. I only make direct eye contact with men that I have found do not try to flirt with me because they are secure in their marriages. With the other men, I look more to the side of them or to the others in the room during a group conversation. This keeps me safe from conveying the wrong message. We also need to avoid being alone with any man that is not our husband.

We need to be careful how we dress. Men are visually stimulated and when we wear tight pants and low-cut tops and other clothes that reveal all our assets, we are causing them to stumble. I believe we are accountable to God for their lustful thoughts. Most Christian men are trying to keep their eyes from looking too long and lusting, but many women in the church today aren't helping them by what they wear to church. Proverbs 11:22 "Like a gold ring in a pig's snout is a beautiful woman who shows no discretion."

If you are a young, single woman reading this, I would like to share with you what I have learned from experience. God designed men to need sex. It is a driving force in the make-up of who they are. If you understand that premise, it will help you realize the motive behind why even Christian men that you may date will try to go as far as they can with you physically. There is a battle raging inside them as they try to obey what Scripture teaches them, but they usually don't know where to draw the line. Then one thing leads to another until *you* draw the line. If you understand that you are probably the one who will tell them to stop, then you can draw that line very early in the process. Don't allow naivety in this area to take you where you don't want to go.

I have had the blessed opportunity to share the following with two different women the week before their wedding night. These two couples did it right. We walked through pre-marital classes with them and they waited to be intimate until their wedding night. Gary had the honored privilege of performing their marriage ceremonies. Our culture conveys that first time sex for the woman is incredible. From most women I have talked to this is not true. You need to first realize that there is a lot of stress and fatigue involved in planning and having a wedding ceremony. This can hit you on your wedding night. Give yourselves permission to sleep first and start fresh at a later time if you both agree to it. Often the week after you get married you might have an emotional breakdown due to all the pent-up stress and exhaustion. This is normal and okay. I know I had an emotional breakdown that week.

God made women more unique sexually. Gary Smalley uses the following word picture: Our bodies are like crock pots that warm up to being sexually stimulated while men are like microwave ovens that warm up instantly. I have found that the female body takes much practice to really respond consistently in all the sexual pleasures. This is especially true when you add in pregnancy and nursing to make things a little more complicated. Just know that your body is normal as you walk this new road of exploration and don't have unrealistic expectations as you adjust to this new adventure in your life.

I'm sure we will all acknowledge that when we start having babies, our stress levels go up and our energy levels and sex drive go down usually due to exhaustion. I think we need to have grace from our husbands while we are at the end of our pregnancies and during the first few months of our babies' lives while we are up every two to three hours of the night and healing from pregnancy and delivery. But it is during all the challenges of birthing our babies and raising young children that we have to work a little harder to maintain our sex life with our husband. This season of life needs to be filled with much grace, but we also can't take advantage of that grace and never meet the needs of our husband. We have to be more creative and even more purposeful to meet their sexual needs. I know we don't feel as sexy during this time because our bodies are usually heavier and babies are nursing and demanding everything from us. These circumstances leave us viewing our husband as just one more person whose needs we have to meet. Be careful to not view him this way. He is also sacrificing during this season and we can't neglect him and his needs for very long without seeing a distance begin in our relationship. Set aside a time to be intimate with him as regularly as you can while you are in this season. We can also work hard to show him love in the other love languages of physical touch and closeness, acts of service, encouraging words, quality time, or gift-giving.

After the kids are older and aren't quite so demanding, our sex life can still be a challenge for us women. Most of us begin to view sex as more of a duty than a pleasure. Bill and Pam Farrel wrote a book entitled: *Men Are Like Waffles, Women Are Like Spaghetti*. We are like spaghetti where everything from our day goes with us into the bedroom. It becomes hard to let it all go and just enjoy our husband sexually. Men, on the other hand, are like waffles and can compartmentalize everything in their day and would have sex even if they knew the world was ending tomorrow. *God purposely made us different.* We need to come to terms with how God made us, but we need to work hard to overcome the things we struggle with so we can have consistent intimacy with our husband.

We need to try to make sure we get enough rest so we will even have the energy to be intimate with our husband. (This seems like it is always a challenge.)

As women we struggle with being the aggressor when it comes to sex, and are usually only the instigator in this area one week a month during the fertile time of our cycle. This is when we should take the opportunity to be the aggressor and make our husband feel wanted sexually. Make every effort to flirt with your husband throughout the day which helps lead into times of intimacy. You can even make dates for when you are both available to have that intimate time together. Planned sex is just as good as spontaneous sex.

Some of you may be in a relationship that is less than fulfilling or you are living with an unbeliever. I know this makes this vulnerable area of sexual intimacy even harder. God sees your obedience and faithfulness and *He will honor it*. Even if your husband does not acknowledge how hard you try to be like Jesus in your actions, Jesus knows and will always be there to help you each step of the way. Lean on Jesus, as you walk in these difficult areas. If there is physical or sexual abuse or extreme verbal/emotional abuse, you must disengage yourself from that relationship to protect you and your children. You must seek professional help from your pastor or a Christian counselor.

> "…If any brother has a wife who does not believe, and she is willing to live with him, let him not divorce her. And a woman who has a husband who does not believe, if he is willing to live with her, let her not divorce him. For the unbelieving husband is sanctified by the wife, and the unbelieving wife is sanctified by the husband; otherwise your children would be unclean, but now they are holy. But if the unbeliever departs, let him depart; a brother or a sister is not under bondage in such cases. But God has called us to peace. For how do you know, O wife, whether you will save your

husband? Or how do you know, O husband, whether you will save your wife?"

I Corinthians 7:12b-16 (*New King James Version*)

GOD DESIGNED SEXUAL INTIMACY
TO BE RESERVED FOR
ONLY OUR HUSBAND.
IT IS WHAT MAKES MARRIAGE
UNIQUE FROM ALL OTHER
RELATIONSHIPS.

CHILDREN ARE A BLESSING! PARENTING IS A MARATHON, NOT A SPRINT!

> "Sons are a heritage from the Lord, children a reward from him. Like arrows in the hands of a warrior are sons born in one's youth. Blessed is the man whose quiver is full of them. They will not be put to shame when they contend with their enemies in the gate." (A quiver was five arrows; God says many children are a blessing.)
>
> Psalm 127:3-5

Proverbs 22:6 "Train a child in the way he should go, and when he is old he will not turn from it." Parenting is such a huge commitment and it is so *daily*. We go over the same life lessons with each of our kids so many times that we feel like a broken record. We have to always remember that parenting is a marathon and the race is eighteen to thirty years long. We also need to have grace for the days when we blow it as parents and we all blow it many times throughout our marathons. But thank God we can start over each day because: "His mercies are new every morning." Lamentations 3:23

I have several friends who have mentally or physically disabled children and one of my sisters has

Turner's syndrome. To all of you sweet parents just keep plugging along as you parent the gifted children God has blessed you with. Your road is paved with extra joys and sometimes harder pains. We all salute you as the specially chosen vessels by God to raise those kids with the love that their Creator has for them. Don't grow weary in well-doing and don't ever feel like a failure because your child seems different or your road seems extremely longer. It is not your fault that they have their special limitations. Don't believe Satan's lies that lead to self-condemnation about what you could have or should have done differently. Just keep loving, training, and caring for these special vessels and know that you are not alone. The truth is you are serving among many of the King's valued soldiers with these special assignments. You will receive your full reward in heaven and hear: "Well done my good and faithful servant!"

I want to share some reminders that I use regularly. *Our kids belong to God. We just get to enjoy loving and raising them for however long He gives them to us.* Just like Moses' parents trusted God to protect their son's life in Exodus chapter two, we must keep an open hand hold on each of our kids with God. He loves them even more than we could because He created each one of them and knows them in every way. God has a plan for each of them and it is our important job to pray for them and prepare them to do the work that God has planned for them to do. *We exercise "faith" by entrusting each of our children to God.*

We are accountable to God for each of their hearts. We need to continue to pursue physical and emotional health for ourselves so that we can offer physical and emotional health to each of our children. We owe it to God, their mates, and society to try to help them achieve maturity in their lives and set them up to succeed as adults. Building maturity into our kids is such a long, hard road. It is tied to their chronological age and how well we, as parents, set the expectation/boundaries in their lives. It requires constant consistency, love, discipline, and encouragement and is not for the faint of heart. But there is a beautiful reward when adults come up to you and tell you that they enjoy your child. It feels like you hit a homerun when your kids love God and worship Him with their actions and life choices. This is when all that hard work pays off. *Never quit as you try to build character into each of your children. You will not see instant results, but you will see results!*

We need to teach them the proper respect and etiquette toward their parents, others, God, their siblings, and themselves. Our culture is not going to teach this to them. It is up to us parents to give them these skills.

We must have *realistic expectations* on ourselves, our husband, and our kids at each stage of the parenting process. This is vital to not being overwhelmed during our parenting marathon. We have to set firm boundaries with our kids while still giving them the freedom to be kids. I am not perfect and I can't expect my kids to be perfect. We have always taught our kids to behave in public and if they needed a place to "lose it" then they should do that at home. Kids need opportunities to "let their hair down" just like we do. Make sure they know when and where that is allowed so they can stay emotionally healthy.

Encourage your kids to become who God wants them to be, not who you want them to be. Help them as they walk their road of discovery and pray for God to show them His perfect will for their lives. I Thessalonians 5:11 "Therefore encourage one another and build each other up, just as in fact you are doing." Also pray for them and for their future spouse that God has planned for each of them.

Make a conscience effort to always hug, kiss, and hold each of your kids even as they become adults. They are still in need of that physical touch as they grow through all the awkward stages of puberty. I know I have to remind myself of this now that they are older whereas when they were little it came very naturally. Moms are designed to nurture small children whereas dads are more equipped to nurture older kids. Use the talents and strengths of both you and your husband during all of the seasons of parenting.

Teach your kids all of the life-skills they will need when they leave your home. They need to know how to cook meals, do laundry, clean the house, mow the lawn, sew, plus everything else you can teach them. Set your kids up to succeed!

We used a Biblical parenting curriculum that helped to guide us through all of our parenting years. Check out their website at www.gfi.org which stands for growing families international. They have teachings for all the ages and stages of our parenting years and it is excellent and affordable.

MAY GOD RICHLY BLESS EACH OF
YOU AS YOU PARENT THE NEXT
GENERATION OF SOLDIERS
FOR CHRIST!

WE ALL HAVE THE SAME KIDS!

> "He who spares the rod hates his son, but he who loves him is careful to discipline him."
>
> Proverbs 13:24

Each of our kids is unique and has a different personality as well as varying difficulties that he/she will face, but the basic steps of growing up are the same. Isn't it fun to get together with other women and hear the same stories about their kids just with a different twist? In fact, it is encouraging for new moms to hear from more experienced moms that what their kid is doing is 'normal.' Especially since our kids do some of the craziest things.

Since we all basically walk the same bases of parenting to make the home run, I want to encourage you to not give up or grow weary in well-doing. You need to focus on the major areas rather than getting so focused on the minor areas that need attention. They need to hear "yes" to things as well as "no." Because of the expectations we have on our kids, we often feel like we are beating our heads against a wall as we train the same thing over and over again. But this is a normal issue in parenting. If you were in elementary school with your children you would realize that the same information is repeated year after year along with some new material. Sometimes, our expectation on our child is unrealistic for their ability level. What I have found regarding those battles, is that I need to back off a little and wait for their chronological maturity to kick in. Then I am able to teach that same lesson to them with less effort and less emotional drain. This applies mostly when they are small children.

> "Foolishness is bound up in the heart of a child, but the rod of discipline will drive it far from him."
>
> Proverbs 22:15

Throughout all of your parenting years your kids will walk through what I call "growth spurts" or "independent streaks." It happens each time they step into another level of maturity/growth development which causes them to stretch their wings of independence. They become more difficult and disobedient. It usually lasts about one to three weeks and you wonder where this "wild child" came from and where your "sweet child" went. This is when you reel them back in and let them know that you are "the boss" and still in control. This is a healthy part of growing up and shouldn't alarm you each time it happens.

We all know about the terrible twos and threes. During this time we have to fight against the strong will in our toddlers to make sure they know that we are the ones in control. There is one more big battle that we have to face and win and that is the puberty years. The puberty years are ages eight to thirteen years old and they will remind you of the battlefield of the toddler years. This puberty battle is one you *must win* in order to enjoy the teen years with your child. We have walked with all four of our kids through this last battle successfully and with much prayer. While their bodies are puberty-changing, their actions resemble the behavior of toddlers. They are more selfish, independent, emotionally unstable, and mean-spirited and think the whole world should revolve around them. And did I mention that *they know it all too!* They allow their peer group or their own naïve thoughts to drive their opinions and they will fight to the end for their view points. This is when you spend hours talking with them and speaking the truths that you know about how life "really" works. They won't receive it initially, but sometime during those four years they will finally listen and surrender. They need to know that you love them and won't abandon them while their peer group will someday abandon them. You'll have some very interesting and exhausting conversations during this season of raising your kids. As they walk this roller-coaster time in their lives, you will have to fight hard and not let them win. This is when you need to maintain strong control in a lovingly firm way and not give in to their whims or when they are teenagers and physically bigger, it will be even harder to reel them back in. Fight hard during the puberty years to stay in control and keep that place of authority in the life of your pre-teen so you can stay their valued parent during their teen years.

Parenting amounts to about a twenty-two year process of letting them go. We go from having total control of their lives as babies, to slowing giving them the age-appropriate tools they need to live life on their own without us. If we can grasp this truth and digest it, then we can emotionally let them go each step of the way. I know this is easier said than done and I have to still walk this road that is right around the corner for me. But I know that in my heart I have been consciously letting my kids grow up and become their own person apart from me through each stage of their development. I believe that by doing this it will be an easier transition for me as they become busy in their own lives as adults.

> "TRAIN UP A CHILD IN THE WAY HE SHOULD GO (*ACCORDING TO HIS OWN BENT*) AND WHEN HE IS OLD… HE WILL NOT TURN FROM IT."
>
> Proverbs 22:6

HOME-SCHOOLING VERSES PUBLIC OR PRIVATE SCHOOLING

God has created us all uniquely and some of us women are designed to be fulfilled in the work force while others are designed to be fulfilled as full-time homemakers. *Be who God made you to be!* Some women have to work to provide for the financial needs of their families and don't have the option of being a full-time homemaker. Whoever God made you to be and whatever your circumstances are, let's not judge the other women who are the opposite of what we are. Let's choose to respect them instead and value the role we each play in society for Christ.

The same is true in the controversy of public verses private schooling verses home-schooling. They all have their place and we need to not judge one another's decision, but instead respect it. All three ways of schooling have their positives and negatives, strengths and weaknesses. The key is to research, pray, and discover which route God is directing your family to take. I know families that go back and forth over the years depending on the circumstances of their lives. Use these options on how to school your kids to your benefit and to the success of your family and parenting.

We chose to home-school our kids because we lived in California where the school systems were so liberal and we wanted them to keep their childhood naivety. We did have our first born in a Christian school for one and a half years but the expense was too much for us. Also, I drove on a field trip while she was in first grade and one of her classmates began to share with the whole car how little babies are made. She used graphic words because her mommy was pregnant and her parents felt free to share that information with their five year old. I asked her to not share anymore in a nice way and realized very quickly how we all have different parenting views.

Later on when Gary was a Christian school administrator, Rachel went to work with Daddy and went to that school and loved it for those two years.

Some of you may be contemplating the idea of home-schooling. I am going to share some of the things I would tell someone who would ask me about what it is like to home-school. The common statement I hear is that, "I could never home-school my kids!" The thought totally overwhelms many people. Then I point out that the time and effort that people spend getting their kids to bed, up early, to and from school, to school functions, and time spent on homework is eliminated and re-directed to time spent schooling your child. This usually makes them relax and have a different thought as to what my world really looks like.

One of my favorite reasons for home-schooling is that I get to see my child grow and change educationally in addition to seeing them change through the development of their character. I love seeing the light bulb of understanding go on in their heads and know that I taught it to them especially when I have been working on something for weeks and they finally get it. I love that I have more time with them to pour in character training in every area of their lives and see it develop daily. They grow up so fast and I feel like I am able to savor more time with them before they enter adulthood.

Home-schooling has proven very beneficial to keeping a more flexible schedule. Gary always worked a fifty to seventy hour work week so I could be a stay-at-home, home-schooling mom. In order for the kids to have time with daddy, we were on a later schedule. As we stepped into full time ministry, this flexible schedule was also a benefit because a lot of ministry is in the evening and we didn't have to worry as much about the kids getting to bed at a certain time in order to get enough sleep. When we need a vacation or time off it is easier because we only have to worry about one person's schedule to coordinate around. Plus we can do a lot of weekday events and not have to fight the crowds as much. Now that our children are older, their more flexible schedule has allowed them the freedom to earn money.

Earlier we discussed how attitude affects everything we do. Home-schooling usually boils down to attitude. At times it was frustrating, but I viewed it as the daily building of character skills into my kids regarding how to face the difficult things in life. There were days when I was at my wits end, and then there were days when all my training/parenting showed. Basically, home-schooling gave me more time to parent our children and teach them how to adjust their attitudes and develop maturity in their lives.

If you are contemplating home-schooling your child, there are many home-school curriculums and options out there today with a variety of price tags and commitment levels. The research can be overwhelming. To those of you who love to research, you'll have a blast deciding what works great for you. For those of you that feel totally overwhelmed by it all, I would suggest you check into two Christian curriculums that we have used and love. For most of our years of home-schooling we used the ABEKA video school. (You can research them at www.abeka.org) I was worried about ruining my kids educationally and them not being able to read, when a friend told me about this video school. They have filmed the whole school year with their "cream-of-the-crop" teachers and they even engage the student watching in their lecture time. They teach everything so well and include a manual for each grade that lays out the daily lesson plans making it so easy to use. These video teachers are who trained me to be the teacher that I am today. I learned so much from them and now use that training to teach preschool to my daycare children. You will spend about $1,000 a year per student using this program. If you feel more confident and can begin by teaching your kids directly, you will spend less than half of that. I think the Abeka curriculum is excellent and has a solid phonics-based and memorization-based model to follow. Another curriculum that we have used is Alpha and Omega which has the option of book form or computer-based teaching called: "Switched on Schoolhouse." You can research them at: www.aophomeschooling.com Alpha and Omega is cheaper than Abeka ranging in the $300–$500 range.

MAY YOU BE BLESSED AS YOU
DISCOVER GOD'S EDUCATIONAL
PLAN FOR EACH OF THE KIDS
IN YOUR FAMILY.

GOD WORKS ALL THINGS TOGETHER FOR GOOD!

> "And we know that in all things God works for the good of those who love him, who have been called according to his purpose."
>
> Romans 8:28

There are times when the circumstances in our lives make it hard for us to believe that God works all things together for good. When we are in the midst of our difficulties, we often times don't see how God is moving or orchestrating the outcome. We can't even see the light at the end of the tunnel. But I hope each one of you have already experienced what it is like to look back on difficult roads you've walked and have seen more clearly God's hand of love, support, and His providence in your life. You see, God knows each of us even better than we know ourselves. He knows the deep areas in each of our hearts that even we are scared to acknowledge or look at. But God's goal for each of us is to help us to heal and grow in all our areas of hurt and immaturity. He also knows what lessons we need to learn for the future events in our lives so we can handle them well when they come.

First, I want to discuss how we live in a fallen world controlled by Satan and our sin nature. When evil things happen, God does not cause them to happen, but He does allow Satan to attack us and He does allow us to walk through the consequences of our choices. Satan causes them to happen. But Satan only has domain on this earth for an appointed time and once his time is over, he will be defeated forever. God wants us to choose to love Him and have an intimate relationship with Him. He has given us *freewill choice*. That freewill choice also prevents Him from forcing man to make right decisions. He will use many means to try to show us the right choices to make, such as His teachings in the Bible or the Holy Spirit convicting our conscience. But each man on earth has the choice to obey His commands or to disobey them. Whenever a person disobeys one of God's commands, another person usually gets hurt in the process. The many injustices that have happened to you have probably left you questioning where God was and why He allowed those events to happen to you. If you ask the Holy Spirit to show you how He was working to be your support and love you through that difficulty, you will be surprised to see all the amazing ways He was actually working. He is always working to touch our lives. Some tools He might use would be through other people, music, financial provision, books, the Bible, or nature to communicate how much He knows and loves you even in the midst of your difficulties.

God hates it when bad things happen to us. He hurts with us and tries to comfort us in a variety of ways. When the source of our pain and affliction is gone and we are left with the wounds, God works to try to help us to heal and restore the damage that was done in our lives. If we press into Him, He will heal every bit of it.

But…the scars will still remain. Jesus' scars from being nailed to the cross still remain. Those scars can then become tools for Him to use in the lives of others who are walking the same road you already walked. This is how He turns it all into good in our lives. Genesis 50:20 "You intended to harm me, but God intended it for good to accomplish what is now being done, the saving of many lives."

Sometimes the bad things that happen are actually what He uses to bring us into a personal relationship with God. My husband's life story really exemplifies this. Gary was born to an eighteen year old mother who got married to escape the unhappy marriage of her parents. She married a man who was twenty-one years old and their marriage lasted only two years. They divorced and Gary went through the parental visitation game for five years. During this time, Gary's mother remarried a wonderful man, Ted Hicks. When Gary was five years old they had Gary's little sister, Shari. Ted legally adopted Gary when he was seven years old. Gary's mother got sick and died when he was ten years old. (She did receive Jesus as her Savior through a TV evangelist while she was sick. These difficult circumstances are also what led Ted to make Jesus Lord of his life as well.) A year after her death, Ted married Gary's 5th grade teacher, Zell. They met at a parent/teacher conference. She had three daughters. Zell is the one who helped get Ted and the kids into church and shortly thereafter Gary also made Jesus his Savior. These two parents, who are both not biological parents, have shaped my husband into the Godly man that he is today. Zell and Gary's four sisters from this blended family taught him how to treat and understand women which was a huge blessing to me when I married him.

God continued working. While we were youth pastors, twenty years after the death of Gary's birth mom, we took our youth to a one week summer camp at Hume Lake, California. Gary was given two boys who were not from our youth group to room with them. One of them was the son of one of the guest speakers and the other one was his friend. Gary happened to share his life story with them when they first met during "room time." Three days later, the friend of that boy got a call from home saying that his mom had gone outside to take out trash and had slipped on the ice and cracked her head open. She didn't live past the next day. When asked whom he wanted to comfort him, he chose Gary because he knew that Gary had lost his mom and would understand more deeply how he felt. Gary was able to minister to that young man effectively because of the loss of his own mother. Doesn't that whole story amaze you of how God works even through difficult circumstances? *The key is time.* We often have to wait many years before we see the multiple ways God is going to use those difficult events in our lives and turn them into good. Just know that *God is faithful and He will do it!*

> TRUST GOD IN ALL YOUR CIRCUMSTANCES TO BRING GOOD FROM THE BAD. HE LOVES TO WORK ALL THINGS FOR HIS GLORY!

WHEN OUR FEAR COLLIDES WITH OUR FAITH!

"The Lord is my light and my salvation—whom shall I fear?
The Lord is the stronghold of my life—of whom shall I be afraid?"

Psalm 27:1

Mark 9:23 "Jesus said, "Everything is possible for him who believes."

You can't have faith if your heart is full of fear. The two don't go together just like oil and water don't mix. Either fear is in control or you are full of faith. Psalm 91:1 says: "The secret of the Lord is with those who fear Him." If we truly fear the Lord rather than our circumstances and trust that our lives are in the control of our loving, heavenly Father, then we must believe that we are safe from the reach of every foe. In Genesis chapter twenty-two, Abraham faced his fear of losing Isaac, his only "covenant son" through Sarah, by obeying in faith the command from God to present Isaac as a living sacrifice on the altar before God. He did not ask man's opinion on God's instruction, he just obeyed. *Our obedience to the Spirit of God in our lives, no matter what the cost, represents a heart full of faith.*

All of our fears tell us that we can't or shouldn't do something. 2 Timothy 1:7 "For God did not give us a spirit of timidity (fear), but a spirit of power, of love and of self-discipline." In order to achieve what God wants us to achieve we have to face those fears head on. Usually, our minds are saying "no" to the things that God has put into our hearts that He wants us to say "yes" to. *Let your heart win!* Don't let your head talk you out of what your heart is saying. There are giants (our fears) in the land. We have to conquer those giants in order to enter the Promised Land. *When God challenges us to change in an area or step out in to the unknown, we must deliberately act!* Even when we feel weak, as soon as we obey God, His almighty power becomes available to us. The feeling of weakness and the temptation of Satan become paralyzed because our act of obedience joins us to God's redemptive power. *It is the action that turns fear into faith!*

> "Therefore, since we have a great high priest who has gone through the heavens, Jesus the Son of God, let us hold firmly to the faith we profess. For we do not have a high priest who is unable to sympathize with our weaknesses, but we have one who has been tempted in every way, just as we are—yet was without sin. Let us then approach the throne of grace with confidence, so that we may receive mercy and find grace in our time of need."
>
> Hebrews 4:14-16

Death is one of those things that we all wrestle with in one way or another. We either fear dying or fear the death of our loved ones or both. Our minds are finite and God is infinite. We can never fully comprehend God, heaven, or eternity. We can only go so far in trying to think about it before our minds shut down, unable to comprehend it all. If you have received Jesus as your Savior, then you know that He already died for your sins so that you no longer have to fear death. Death does not mean eternal death anymore. With Jesus as our Savior, we walk through the door of death into eternal life. That life is perfect and never-ending; the way God always wanted it to be with us before man chose to sin and eat the forbidden fruit and became separated from God. Eternal life is where there are no more tears or heartache or difficulties. I know that when I'm in the middle of hard times, it makes me long for heaven where I won't have to worry about all my difficulties anymore. The hardest thing for my finite mind to try to comprehend is God Himself. What I have learned about Him here on earth is only a small fraction of whom He fully is. The deep love I feel from Him is also only a small fraction of how I will feel when I stand in His presence. These things have helped to take away a lot of my fear of death. I wrestle more with the fear of losing loved ones and how hard it will be to be left behind without them. They will be fine in heaven because they know Jesus, but I will miss them so much until I get to join them there. So far for me, my sweet Gramie is in heaven with Jesus and I miss her. I know she is laughing at me. She lived in Texas while we lived in California all these years and after she went to heaven was when God moved us to Texas. I know she's teasing me saying, "Now, you move to Texas!"

Sickness is another circumstance that is hard for us to understand. It is so painful and keeps us from fulfilling our life responsibilities. At times it makes us feel like we are a burden on our loved ones. Let's look past those initial thoughts and see more how God sees it.

1. Sickness can be used by God as a tool to get us out of the rat-race of life and give us time to focus on our relationship with Him or focus more on our loved ones.

2. Sickness makes us appreciate health rather than take it for granted. It makes us value at a deeper level each moment that we get to enjoy of this life on earth because we begin to re-focus our perspective on life.

3. God brings beauty out of the ashes of our lives. I know of a woman who while fighting cancer wrote two children's books during that hard time in her life. I've read many stories about other women who are blind or bed-ridden and chose to use their limitations to become incredible intercessors for the body of Christ.

John 11:4 "When he heard this, Jesus said, "This sickness will not end in death. *No, it is for God's glory so that God's Son may be glorified through it."* Whether our sickness is temporary or does end in death, God can be glorified through it all. This past 3 years our family has walked through major illness with Gary, my husband. It has been very, very hard at times. I can honestly tell you that God has been faithful in every way from helping pay for the two hospital stays and Doctor Bills; to giving all of us the strength to walk this road, and helping us to see God get the glory in and through the entire process. God never abandoned us and we all saw Him working at each turn in the road even if we didn't like walking the road. Many wonderful things have come out of these years and we thank God for being our strong tower through it all.

> Oswald Chambers in his book, *Daily Thoughts for Disciples,* shares these incredible thoughts. Job 13:15 "Though He slay me, yet will I trust Him." *"We sometimes wrongly illustrate faith in God by the faith of a businessperson in a bind. Faith commercially is based on calculation, but religious faith cannot be illustrated by the kind of faith we exhibit in life. Faith in God is a terrific venture in the dark; I have to believe that God is good in spite of all that contradicts it in my experience. It is not easy to say that God is love when everything that happens actually gives the lie to it. Everyone's soul represents some kind of battlefield. The point for each one is whether he or she will hang on, as Job did, and say, "Though things look black, I will trust in God."…*
>
> *The basis of faith in God is that God is the Source and Support of all existence, not that He is all existence. Job recognizes this, and maintains that in the end everything will be explained and*

made clear. Have I this kind of faith—not faith in a principle, but faith in God, *that He is just and true and right?"*

Faith is a gift from God and can only come from Him. Whenever I have given into my fears and do not have faith, I ask the Holy Spirit to come and fill me with His faith. He has always honored that request. Try it and see Him change your heart in each circumstance as it arises. Another tip that helps me when I am struggling to overcome my fear and become full of faith and victorious is to begin worshipping God through song. As I worship Him, my burden begins to lift and so does my fear. Hebrews 11:1 "Now faith is being sure of what we hope for and certain of what we do not see."

> *"Faith, mighty faith, the promise sees, and looks to God alone; laughs at impossibilities, and cries it shall be done."*
>
> —Charles Wesley

TRY TO VIEW FAITH AS A MUSCLE
THAT NEEDS TO BE EXERCISED
IN ORDER TO GROW BIGGER AND
STRONGER.
IT IS A LIFE LONG PROCESS…AND
WORTH THE PRACTICE.

ADVERSITY: GOD'S TOOL TO MATURE US

"Be self-controlled and alert. Your enemy the devil prowls around like a roaring lion looking for someone to devour. Resist him, standing firm in the faith, because you know that your brothers throughout the world are undergoing the same kind of sufferings. And the God of all grace, who called you to his eternal glory in Christ, after you have suffered a little while, will himself restore you and make you strong, firm and steadfast. To Him be the power for ever and ever. Amen.

I Peter 5:8-11

"Blessed are you when people insult you, persecute you and falsely say all kinds of evil against you because of me. Rejoice and be glad, because great is your reward in heaven, for in the same way they persecuted the prophets who were before you.

Matthew 5:11-12

"If you faint in the day of adversity, your strength is small."

Proverbs 24:10

We all hate adversity yet it is one of God's favorite tools to shape and mold us into His image. We all have prayed prayers asking God to make us more like Him, or to give us patience etc. Then difficult things begin to happen and we scratch our heads in confusion. God is answering our prayers. I have found that much of the adversity that God uses to mature me is through adversity with people. It comes in a variety of ways and the circumstances are never the same, but the pain infused into my life has the same results. When people get mad or offended with us for no good reason, it hurts us deeply. This is the process He uses to chisel off our rough edges and break us in order to make us more loving and compassionate toward others who experience similar things.

Initially, we naively only expect these difficulties to come from the ungodly, but then we get side-swiped by the people in the body of Christ and we are left disillusioned and confused. This is God working at an even deeper level. When we are treated unfairly by fellow Christians, we must understand that God is cutting even deeper into our souls and using those hurtful words and actions to re-shape our mind, will and emotions to become more like Him. Jesus was betrayed by his close friend Judas, one of his twelve disciples. We will also be betrayed by close friends in the body of Christ. Over my forty-four years, three different close girl friends have walked away from our friendship… and I didn't feel like I did anything to deserve it. But God used each event in my life to continue to soften my heart for others and to teach me how to suffer with Him in the same sufferings that He endured. God has taught me how to let go of people who walk away because I now understand that they are ultimately His responsibility, not mine. I am only accountable to God for my actions; not theirs. I must choose to continue to love them and forgive them just like Jesus did. Betrayal is always a very difficult adversity. Allow Jesus to walk with you each step of the way down that very painful road. Remember, He has already traveled it before us. Out of the three friends, one of them has restored our relationship, and God's goal of a full-circle restoration is so beautiful!

> "It was good for me to be afflicted so that I might learn your decrees. The law from your mouth is more precious to me than thousands of pieces of silver and gold. Your hands made me and formed me; give me understanding to learn your commands. May those who fear you rejoice when they see me, for I have put my hope in your Word. I know, O Lord, that your laws are righteous, and in faithfulness you have afflicted me. May your unfailing love be my comfort, according to your promise to your servant. Let your compassion come to me that I may live, for your law is my delight. May the arrogant be put to shame for wronging me without cause; but I will meditate on your precepts. May those who fear you turn to me, those who understand your statutes. May my heart be blameless toward your decrees, that I may not be put to shame."
>
> Psalm 119:71-80

Adversity comes in many ways such as financial struggle, divorce, sickness, abandonment, slander, or rejection to name a few. Each one originates from Satan and his tactics, but God always comes in to save the day and make His "good" come out of the bad. Each time adversity strikes, we have the choice to either become bitter or better. When we choose bitterness we allow the difficulties to lead us down the path that leads us to discouragement and failure. Bitterness leaves us victimized by our adversary. When we choose to become better through our difficulties the trial becomes a challenge from God to claim a larger blessing than we ever could have expected. It becomes the avenue used to obtain a larger measure of God's divine grace. This is when Satan's tactics become the force that pushes us toward the furtherance of God's plan in our life. Surely, we are more than conquerors through Him who loves us!

Jesus is the vine, we are the branches, and God is the vine dresser. He knows where to plant us, when to fertilize us, and when to water us. But He also knows when to *prune* us and precisely where to cut us. We have to trust in His skill and knowledge of who we are and who He is making us to become. Only vines and branches that have been pruned precisely bear *much fruit* during harvest-time. The rich, sweet, full fruit in our lives is worth whatever the vine dresser allows to shape and mold us so that we may be used more mightily for His glory. John 15:5 "I am the vine; you are the branches. If a man remains in me and I in him, he will bear much fruit; apart from me you can do nothing." John 15:8 "This is to my Father's glory, that you bear much fruit, showing yourselves to be my disciples." Always remember that just like there are four weather seasons, we walk through various seasons in our lives. If you are currently in a winter season keep in mind that the colder the winter is…the more bugs it kills which helps the next season of spring to be more fruitful. Winter never lasts forever! Thank you, Lord!

Lastly, we all want to be used by God to love people for His kingdom and glory. The road of adversity helps us to become more compassionate toward others as we watch them walk the same road we have endured. We become able to brush off idle words or untruths more easily and quickly. We become filled with Jesus' love and compassion. We begin to see through the circumstances to the motive of their attack which could be insecurity, fear of rejection, or just lies of the enemy. Then the Holy Spirit will help us to pray for them to be healed in those hurting areas of their lives. As you experience these new Christ-like reactions, there is only one explanation for why you are responding accordingly: GOD! *God is in control and using you to love hurting people the same way He loves them.* God sees people in all their sin and failures and looks on them with deep love and compassion as He works to reach them with His love. Now your prayers of being used for His glory and becoming Christ-like are being answered as He births His kind of love and compassion in your heart. *Oswald Chambers writes in My Utmost For His Highest: "If you are going to be used by God, He will take you through a number of experiences that are not meant for you personally at all. They are designed to make you useful in His hands, and to enable you to understand what takes place in the lives of others. Because of this process, you will never be surprised by what comes your way. You say, "Oh, I can't deal with that person." Why can't you? God gave you sufficient opportunities to learn from Him about that problem."…We never realize at the time what God is putting us through—we go through it more or less without understanding. Then suddenly we come to a place of enlightenment, and realize—"God has strengthened me and I didn't even know it!"* God is an expert in making us into tools that He can use in the lives of others later on.

As with everything else, God's ways are not our ways. The road to unconditional love is through adversity. Always remember that He never requires you to walk this road alone. The poem "Footprints in the Sand" talks about how Jesus walks by our side every step of the way. There are also times when we only see one set of footprints. That is the time that He is carrying us. This road is painful and requires us to die to ourselves as we surrender to all that God is trying to do in us. John 12:24 "I tell you the truth, unless a kernel of wheat falls to the ground and dies, it remains only a single seed. But if it dies, it produces many seeds." Just like a seed must die in the earth before it can bring forth a great harvest, we must die to ourselves, in order to reap a huge harvest for our King of Kings and Lord of Lords.

As we enter the end times, many of us probably fear that we will have to face martyrdom for our faith. I know this is something I have thought about. The conclusion I have come to from listening to stories of people who have faced martyrdom is that I believe the Holy Spirit will fill us with a supernatural strength to face that very difficult circumstance and usher us into His presence in a unique way.

KEEP LEANING ON JESUS…
THE AUTHOR AND FINISHER
OF YOUR FAITH!

GOD (*DISCIPLES*) DISCIPLINES THOSE HE LOVES!

"My son, do not make light of the Lord's discipline, and do not lose heart when he rebukes you, because the Lord disciplines those he loves, and he punishes everyone he accepts as a son. Endure hardship as discipline; God is treating you as sons. For what son is not disciplined by his father? If you are not disciplined (and everyone undergoes discipline), then you are illegitimate children and not true sons. Moreover, we have all had human fathers who disciplined us and we respected them for it. How much more should we submit to the Father of our spirits and live! Our fathers disciplined us for a little while as they thought best; *but God disciplines us for our good, that we may share in his holiness. No discipline seems pleasant at the time, but painful. Later on, however, it produces a harvest of righteousness and peace for those who have been trained by it.*"

Hebrews 12:5b-11

How many of you allow your kids to fail at something in order to use it as an opportunity to teach them the truth or the right way to handle those circumstances. As you know, it takes self-control as a parent to let our kids fail. It is also painful to watch. We often watch them disobey something we have taught them and then we discipline them with the consequences of those choices. Some consequences are from the "laws that be" such as the law of gravity. We tell them not to run in rugged terrain; they disobey, fall and get hurt. We teach them how to treat others in a nice way; they choose to be mean to their friend and their friend stops playing with them. Then there are the consequences that we enforce on our kids to help them mature. Sometimes our discipline is a spanking, grounding, loss of a privilege, or a time out. Often this is hard for us to do because it is hard to watch them suffer and most kids lay huge guilt trips on their parents while they are suffering. But we know, as adults, that painful consequences are the only way to cause our kids to learn and grow. No pain, no gain applies to us physically as well as in the maturing process of life.

This is the same way God works with us. He knows the areas in which we are being stubborn and disobedient and He allows the "laws that be" to discipline us as well as "His consequences" in order to teach us His ways. His goal is that we will mature and grow closer to Him and become more like Him each day. We must learn from our mistakes in order to grow. Then as we learn each lesson, He brings along a testing opportunity to see whether or not we will truly make the right choice when faced with the same circumstance. *God loves to test our character!* He cares about the little things in our character. I recently backed into a car parked across the street at our neighbor's house. I knew that I had to go and knock on the door and tell them what I had done and see how they wanted to proceed, but I dreaded doing it. After I knocked on the door, a tall, buff man answered the door and it was his car. He was a friend visiting from out of town. Luckily, his car could be buffed out while my car had the dent and he said it was fine. What a relief! I could have chosen to not tell him, but my conscience would have killed me with conviction. I felt in my spirit that God was testing me to see if I would make the right decision in this awkward situation.

I view this process in my life with a word picture of the potter and the clay. My life is on God's spinning wheel and He is trying to make me into fine china. If I don't conform to the shaping of His hands, He may get me wet all over again, roll me into a ball, and start over again. He never throws me away, but He will allow new avenues to teach me the same lesson that I refused to learn previously. Then as I progress enough to look like a tea cup, I have to go into the fiery furnace to set. But are you aware that fine china must be fired at least three times and occasionally it is fired more than three times? The firing is necessary to make the gold and crimson shine more beautifully and permanently. The key to surviving this process is to understand that "God is our refuge and strength, a very present *help in trouble.*" Psalm 46:1 First He will help us and teach us *in* our trouble as He shapes and molds us into His image. Then after we surrender to all He is teaching us and we become calm and quiet under the strain of pain, He will deliver us out of it.

> "So if you think you are standing firm, be careful that you don't fall! No temptation has seized you except what is common to man. And God is faithful; he will not let you be tempted beyond what you can bear. But when you are tempted, he will also provide a way out so that you can stand up under it."
>
> I Corinthians 10:12-13

As we continue to grow in our walks with Christ, our testing gets harder, just like the testing gets harder with our kids as they get older. The consequences of a toddler throwing a fit are totally different than the consequences of an eighteen year old having an attitude with a teacher or policeman. Likewise, our spiritual trials and testing become harder and more painful. This is especially true when it is a lesson that we refuse to learn. God will continue to bring different circumstances into our lives to try to teach us that lesson. I try to submit to His teaching the first time to avoid having to learn the lesson through a harder situation later on which is what I call: "Taking another lap!" When the Israelites left Egypt, they were only eleven days away from Canaan, but instead it took them forty years to arrive there. They kept grumbling, complaining and disobeying God. After many opportunities for them to begin trusting God to take care of them, He finally punished them with forty years in the desert until all of the stubborn people died out. They had to keep traveling the same desert over and over again without ever entering the "promised land." As I first read from Exodus through Deuteronomy my response was, "How can these people be so stupid and stubborn?" Then when I read it while I was struggling through something God was trying to teach me, I begin to realize that I am just like them…stupid and stubborn. Sounds like all of us! On a different note, sometimes God will take us into the desert, a quiet place that is free of distractions, so that we can *clearly hear* what He is trying to tell us.

> "Dear friends, do not be surprised at the painful trial you are suffering, as though something strange were happening to you. But rejoice that you participate in the sufferings of Christ, so that you may be overjoyed when his glory is revealed. If you are insulted because of the name of Christ, you are blessed, for the Spirit of glory and of God rests on you. If you suffer, it should not be as a murderer or thief or any other kind of criminal, or even as a meddler. However, if you suffer as a Christian, do not be ashamed, but praise God that you bear that name. For it is time for judgment to begin with the family of God; and if it begins with us, what will the outcome be for those who do not obey the gospel of God? And, "If it is hard for the righteous to be saved, what will become of the ungodly and sinner?" So then, those who suffer according to God's will should commit themselves to their faithful Creator and continue to do good."
>
> I Peter 4:12-19

This powerful analogy explains how this process works in our lives.

"A bar of steel worth five dollars, when wrought into horseshoes, is worth ten dollars. If made into needles, it is worth $350; if into penknife blades, it is worth $32,000; if into springs for watches it is worth $250,000. What a drilling the poor bar must undergo to be worth this! But the more it is manipulated, the more it is hammered, and passed through the fire, and beaten and pounded and polished, the greater the value.

May this parable help us to be silent, still, and long-suffering. Those who suffer most are capable of yielding most; and it is through pain that God is getting the most out of us, for His glory and the blessing of others."

—Selected Streams in the Desert 10/24

"Blessed is the man whom God corrects; so do not despise the discipline of the Almighty. For He wounds, but He also binds up; He injures, but His hands also heal."

Job 5:17-18

GOD IS MAKING US INTO HIS PURE/SPOTLESS BRIDE! THIS TAKES DISCIPLINE AND TESTINGS…TO HELP US BECOME MORE LIKE HIM!

GOD'S "WAITING ROOM"

> "But do not forget this one thing, dear friends: With the Lord a day is like a thousand years, and a thousand years are like a day. The Lord is not slow in keeping his promise, as some understand slowness. He is patient with you, not wanting anyone to perish, but everyone to come to repentance."
>
> 2 Peter 3:8-9

Proverbs 29:18 "Where there is no vision, the people perish." God will first fill our heart and mind with an incredible vision of the future of our life with Him. Then one of God's favorite tests He uses with His more mature children is to "wait." Usually those delays come with suffering, but through it all He promises to never leave us or forsake us. The truth is that the delays and suffering are part of His promised blessing because as we wait on Him He will strengthen our hearts and fill us with courage to keep walking by faith and not by sight. It often feels like we just *hurry up…and wait*! We get excited and motivated to accomplish the vision God has given us, only to have to stop and wait for His perfect timing while He is preparing us for the vision. This is an area that I often struggle with. Isaiah 49:23 "They shall not be ashamed that wait for me."

Abraham could not understand why God would ask him to sacrifice his long awaited "covenant" son; but he chose to trust and obey and saw the glory of God arrive at the end of "his" test of obedience. (Genesis 21-22) Hebrews 6:15 "And so after waiting patiently, Abraham received what was promised."

Joseph was promised power and authority in his God-given dreams. The strong jealousy his brothers had toward him caused them to sell him into slavery in Egypt. Potipher made Joseph his valued slave after seeing how God blessed everything he did. While he was there Potipher's wife tried to get Joseph to be intimate with her. When he refused and tried to escape her advances, she lied about what really happened which then landed him in prison. It seemed his Godly actions only landed him in more trouble. There he waited even longer for God to fulfill the dreams He had given to him. After more waiting, God gloriously fulfilled the promised vision by giving Joseph the interpretation of Pharoah's prophetic dreams. This led to Pharoah making Joseph second-in-command of Egypt where God used him to save lives during the famine, including the lives of his family. (Genesis 39-41) *The greater the vision or dream God has called us to fulfill, the greater the training and waiting will be in order to purify our motives and shift our dependence to be only on God rather than ourselves.*

God had given Joseph prophetic dreams, and then He took Joseph through many years of training and testing to prepare Joseph for the fulfillment of those dreams. God was faithful to the vision he gave Joseph and He *will be faithful* to the vision He has placed in your heart. I Peter 5:6-7 "Humble yourselves, therefore, under God's mighty hand, that he may lift you up in due time. Cast all your anxiety on him because he cares for you."

Moses knew God had called him to save his people from slavery in Egypt. But he took matters into his own hands, and in his attempt to defend his people, he killed an Egyptian taskmaster. Fear of consequences at the hand of Pharaoh led Moses into exile for forty years of waiting and training where God made him into the Godly leader he needed to become. When God's timing was right, Moses trusted and obeyed God and saw Him gloriously deliver the Israelites from the slavery of the Egyptians to the brink of the Promised Land; led by the glory cloud of God Himself. You will notice in this story that when Moses thought he was ready he was not. Then when God said Moses was ready, he did not at all feel ready for the assignment. There is something wonderful about this "waiting room" process that gets us to the end of ourselves; to the end of thinking we can do something great for God. Instead we realize that we can do nothing in or of ourselves. We learn the truth that all we have to offer is only because of God working in and through us. This shift is so freeing and amazing as we stand in awe that He would use one such as me in any way for His glory. (Exodus 2-15) Isaiah 30:18 "Blessed are all they that wait for Him."

We usually are in God's "waiting room" for the following two reasons. 1. He is waiting until we are ready by maturing us for the task ahead. 2. We are waiting until He is ready—the perfect timing of His promised plans. Forces of time and circumstance must be in effect in order to see the fruition of the promised vision. There are times when God's delays are purposeful…because the delay plays into the fulfillment of the answer to the prayer. In God's plan... *TIMING is everything!*

> *"Waiting is much more difficult than walking. Waiting requires patience, and patience is a rare virtue. It is fine to know that God builds hedges around His people—when the hedge is looked at from the viewpoint of protection. But when the hedge is kept around one until is grows so high that he cannot see over the top, and wonders whether he is ever to get out of the little sphere of influence and service in which he is pent up, it is hard for him sometimes to understand why he may not have a larger environment—hard for him to "brighten the corner" where he is. But God has a purpose in all HIS holdups.* Psalm 37:23 "The steps of a good man are ordered by the Lord." *On the margin of his Bible at this verse George Mueller had a notation, "And the stops also." It is a sad mistake for men to break through God's hedges. It is a vital principle of guidance for a Christian never to move out of the place in which he is sure God has placed him, until the Pillar of Cloud moves."*
>
> —From Sunday School Times
> Streams in the Desert 8/16

"Be patient, then, brothers, until the Lord's coming. See how the farmer waits for the land to yield its valuable crop and how patient he is for the autumn and spring rains. You too, be patient and stand firm, because the Lord's coming is near."

James 5:7-8

Coffee Talk

It has been said that there are many black dots in each of our lives and we don't know why they are there. Their presence doesn't make any sense to us. Why did God allow this or that to happen? Then we have the times of waiting that leave us even more confused and frustrated. If we can step back and look at our lives through God's vantage point, we will see the bigger picture. We will all be surprised to see the black dots representing music notes perfectly placed on the page. He draws lines to connect each note accordingly and puts *rests* in at the proper time to make a perfect and glorious harmony in our lives.

> IT HELPS IF WE VIEW *WAITING* AS THE ACTION VERB THAT IT IS. WAITING REQUIRES THE SAME EFFORT AS WORKING DOES.

DON'T GIVE UP! LIFE IS HARD...BUT GOD IS GOOD!

> "To keep me from becoming conceited because of these surpassingly great revelations, there was given me a thorn in my flesh, a messenger of Satan, to torment me. Three times I pleaded with the Lord to take it away from me. But he said to me, "My grace is sufficient for you, for my power is made perfect in weaknesses." Therefore I will boast all the more gladly about my weaknesses, so that Christ's power may rest on me. That is why, for Christ's sake, I delight in weaknesses, in insults, in hardships, in persecutions, in difficulties. For when I am weak, then I am strong."
>
> 2 Corinthians 12:7-10

We all have difficulties in our lives. One struggle, in particular, may feel like a 'thorn' similar to what Paul experienced. Biblical commentators suggest that it was malaria, epilepsy, or a disease of the eyes. Whatever it was, it was a hindrance that made Paul's life and ministry more difficult.

Three times Paul asked God to take it away from him. Have you asked God to remove something from you life many times and the answer has always been "no"? Be encouraged with God's answer: "My grace IS sufficient for you, for my power is made perfect in weakness." In the middle of the hard times, God's grace and power will be there for us to use. These very hard things in our lives are used to keep us humble and *dependant* on God. It is a gift from God to keep us from being puffed up with pride and independent of Him. Through our afflictions God can demonstrate His power. He can do this if we *rely on Him* for our effectiveness rather than on our own abilities and talents. "Therefore I will boast all the more gladly about my weaknesses, so that Christ's power may rest on me." These weaknesses are God's tools that He uses to build character in each of our lives. As we admit our weaknesses and affirm that God is our strength, we then become dependent on Him. Dependence on someone means we trust them. As we depend on God, and see Him make us strong through our weaknesses we begin to worship and praise Him for those weaknesses. This is something we desire with our husbands as well. We want to feel safe and secure in our weak areas. We want to depend on our mate to protect us from harm when those weaknesses arise. If you can see how we do this with our physical lover, it will be easier to understand how you can do this with the author and lover of your soul.

> "As you know, we consider blessed those who have persevered. You have heard of Job's perseverance and have seen what the Lord finally brought about. The Lord is full of compassion and mercy."
>
> James 5:11

> *"Job's greatest test was not the pain, but that he did not know <u>why</u> he was suffering. Our greatest test may be that we must trust God's goodness even though we don't understand why our lives are going a certain way. We must learn to trust in God who is good and not in the goodness of life."*
>
> —*NIV Life Application Bible commentary on Job 33:13.*

As you know, this is easier said than done. Reading about the life experiences of Job may help you as you wrestle with the *why* of your circumstances. Allow God to help you to trust in His goodness rather than in the goodness of life.

> *"Suffering is a wonderful fertilizer to the roots of character. The great object of this life is character. This is the only thing we can carry with us into eternity...."*
>
> —*Austin Phelps Streams in the Desert 12/2*

There are no short cuts to the life of faith. It requires walking the narrow pathway of suffering to build our character in Christ. Joshua 1:9 says: "Have I not commanded you? Be strong and courageous. Do not be terrified; do not be discouraged, for the Lord your God will be with you wherever you go."

> *There is a poem called "The Changed Cross." It represents a weary one who thought that her cross was surely heavier than those of others whom she saw about her, and she wished that she might choose another instead of her own. She slept, and in*

her dream she was led to a place where many crosses lay, crosses of different shapes and sizes. There was a little one most beauteous to behold, set in jewels and gold. "Ah, this I can wear with comfort," she said. So she took it up, but her weak form shook beneath it. The jewels and the gold were beautiful, but they were far too heavy for her.

Next she saw a lovely cross with fair flowers entwined around its sculptured form. Surely that was the one for her. She lifted it, but beneath the flowers were piercing thorns which tore her flesh.

At last, as she went on, she came to a plain cross, without jewels, without carvings, with only a few words of love inscribed upon it. This she took up and it proved the best of all, the easiest to be borne. And as she looked upon it, bathed in the radiance that fell from heaven, she recognized her own old cross. She had found it again, and it was the best of all and lightest for her.

God knows best what cross we need to bear. We do not know how heavy it is. Here is another whose life seems very lovely. She bears a cross twined with flowers. If we could try all the other crosses that we think lighter than our own, we would at last find that not one of them suited us so well as our own.

—From Glimpses through Life's Windows
Streams in the Desert 8/29

God knows what weakness or thorn in our flesh that each one of us can handle. He knows what 'life experience' we will need to accomplish His divine plan for our lives. Trust Him! He is a Master craftsman at shaping us into the perfect vessels to be used for His glory.

> "Do you not know that in a race all the runners run, but only one gets the prize? Run in such a way as to get the prize. Everyone who competes in the game goes into strict training. They do it to get a crown that will not last; but we do it to get a crown that will last forever. Therefore I do not run like a man running aimlessly; I do not fight like a man beating the air. No, I beat my body and make it my slave so that after I have preached to others, I myself will not be disqualified for the prize."
>
> I Corinthians 9:24-27

We all need each other to finish the race. This is where everything we have been discussing comes into play. We are not designed to do this alone. We need the help of God and fellow Christians to help us walk our road and understand the things we are experiencing. God uses others who have already experienced what you are experiencing to help you know that you are not alone and that you can make it through. If you don't avail yourself of God's help and the help of others you will give up and quit. Lions use the following hunting strategy to catch their meat. They hunt in a pack. They cannot pick off a weaker animal that is traveling in a herd. So they try to divert one of the stragglers from the herd so they can gang up on it and eat it. This is what Satan does to us if we let him. Don't allow him to divert you from other believers and become a lone straggler that he can pick off and destroy.

> "God is not unjust; He will not forget your work and the love you have shown Him as you have helped His people and continue to help them. We want each of you to show this same diligence to the very end, in order to make your hope sure. We do not want you to become lazy, but to imitate those who through faith and patience inherit what has been promised."
>
> Hebrews 6:10-12

LET US NOT BECOME WEARY IN DOING GOOD, FOR AT THE PROPER TIME WE WILL REAP A HARVEST IF WE DON'T GIVE UP.

Galatians 6:9

TAKE ME! BLESS ME! CRUSH ME! USE ME!

> "Surely he will never be shaken; a righteous man will be remembered forever. He will have no fear of bad news; his heart is steadfast, trusting in the Lord. His heart is secure, he will have no fear; in the end he will look in triumph on his foes."
>
> Psalm 112:6-8

In order to be mightily used by God we have to first be mightily crushed! Through crushing we become broken bread and poured out wine for others to feed on as we are used to help them grow up in their walks with Christ. This principle is all over Scripture. God did this with Abraham, Jacob, Joseph, Moses, David, Jesus, and Paul to name a few. Let's use David as our example to illustrate this process. You can read about his incredible story in the books of I & II Samuel.

Take me, Lord! David surrendered his life and service to God as a young boy and God used that time to show David how deeply He loved him. He was able to perform mighty feats for God as a shepherd, like killing a lion and other animals who threatened his sheep. During this time in David's life he wrote some beautiful psalms about God and His love and faithfulness to those who obey His laws. The "Take Me" season is when you see and feel the tangible evidence of God's intimate love in your life. This is usually when God downloads the vision He has for your life. This is when David was anointed as the next king of Israel by Samuel, the prophet of God. It was an amazing time in David's young life. All of these events caused David to step out in bold faith, dependant on his faithful God. He was the only one who stepped up to face the terrifying giant, Goliath. His God would deliver Goliath into David's hands and give victory to the Israelites through him. This victory propelled David into:

Bless me, Lord! Enjoy this season while you are in it. The fruit of David's bold faith in God launched him into an incredible season of blessing. He was given the king's daughter in marriage and wealth. What an honor! He met his best friend, Prince Jonathan, and cultivated that deep friendship. He became the head of Saul's army and led the Israelites from victory to victory against the Philistines. He was undefeatable! But his success caused the people to praise him above King Saul which sent David spiraling downward into the next season:

Crush me, Lord! King Saul's jealousy, along with an evil spirit, caused him to throw a spear at David twice; he sent David into the front lines of battle to get the foreskins of 200 Philistines hoping that he would be killed; he tried to get Jonathan and the attendants to kill David; he tried to pin him to the wall with a spear again; he tried to murder him in his own bed; he tried again to get Jonathan to bring David to him so he could kill him. Saul and his army chased David and his men all over Israel trying to kill them for many years.

Doesn't that sound like crushing circumstances to you? The following verse is the last conversation between David and Jonathan. I Samuel 20:41b "Then they kissed each other and wept together—but David wept the most." Why do you think scripture would include this statement that David wept the most? Because he had just lost EVERYTHING! There are many stories of David's successes and failures during this season of crushing. He mostly acted in ways that honored God, but he had his mistakes too. But God always helped him out of those mistakes. David was being crushed and molded into a powerful leader for God and for Israel. He was being tried and tested by God to see what David was made of. All of the adversities were designed to fill David with the character and compassion needed to be the first great king Israel had ever known. Plus his lineage became the lineage of Christ, the Son of God. *Remember: To be mightily used, we have to be mightily crushed!* David wrote many psalms asking God to 'avenge him' or asking 'where God was' during this season of his life. Even as we walk through the end of our crushing season, it is still full of difficulties. King Saul and Jonathan were killed in battle, yet only Judah instated David as King at this time. David had to wait another seven and a half years and walk through a different kind of crushing before he was made king of all Israel: 2 Samuel 3:1 "The war between the house of Saul and the house of David lasted a long time. David grew stronger and stronger, while the house of Saul grew weaker and weaker."

Use me, Lord! Finally, David was made king over all of Israel and he reigned over Israel and Judah for thirty-three years. David still made mistakes along the way, but he was an incredible king due to all the things he had learned during his crushing time. God uses us by giving us away to bless and feed others at this stage in the process.

During our times of crushing, it feels like life is no longer worth living. It forces us to admit that we have offenses with God because He did not act the way we thought He should or would. It causes our areas of immaturity to rise to the surface. This is when we face the daily test of whether we are going to 'give up' or 'press on in faith.' We have so many personal stories from our own lives that show God working in these ways. At the time, it is so painful and it feels like it is more than we can bear. Both Gary and I contemplated giving up on the vision God had given us and quitting, but that really should never be an option. Life in disobedience to God is an unfulfilled existence. Instead, after we have walked through the crushing times, we then get to see the beautiful fruit that it produces in our lives. This is the fruit that we wanted and even asked God for. This is when we firmly decide that we wouldn't trade the pain or the crushing for anything because we are stronger and wiser and have more depth because of it. The crushing brings us to a new, deeper level of unwavering trust in God's providential hand in our life. I hope it helps us all to know that we are not alone in our trials and testing. God is working in these ways with each one of us. (Sermon taught by Les Beauchamp)

"Oh, the depth of the riches of the wisdom and knowledge of God!

How unsearchable are his judgments, and his paths beyond tracing out!

Who has known the mind of the Lord? Or who has been his counselor?

Who has ever given to God, that God should repay him?

For from him and through him and to him are all things.

To him be the glory forever! Amen.

Romans 11:33-36

"When God wants to drill a man,
and thrill a man, and kill a man;
When God wants to skill a man
to play the noblest part.
When He yearns with all His heart
to create so great and bold a man;
That all the world will be amazed…watch
His methods…watch His ways.
How He ruthlessly perfects whom
He royally elects.
How He hammers him and hurts him and
with mighty blows converts him;
In to trial shapes of clay which only God
understands?
While his tortured heart is crying and
he lifts beseeching hands.
How he bends but never breaks when
His good He undertakes.
How He uses whom He chooses,
and with every purpose fuses him;

By every act induces him to try
God's splendor out.
GOD KNOWS WHAT HE IS ABOUT!"

—Author Unknown

GLORIFY GOD WHILE YOU ARE IN
THE FIRES OF YOUR LIFE!

GOD KNOWS AND WALKS WITH EACH OF US INDIVIDUALLY!

"O Lord, you have searched me and you know me. You know when I sit and when I rise; you perceive my thoughts from afar. You discern my going out and my lying down; you are familiar with all my ways. Before a word is on my tongue you know it completely, O Lord. You hem me in—behind and before; you have laid your hand upon me. Such knowledge is too wonderful for me, too lofty for me to attain. Where can I go from your Spirit? Where can I flee from your presence? If I go up to the heavens, you are there; if I make my bed in the depths, you are there. If I rise on the wings of the dawn, if I settle on the far side of the sea, even there your hand will guide me; your right hand will hold me fast. If I say, "Surely the darkness will hide me and the light become night around me, even the darkness will not be dark to you; the night will shine like the day, for darkness is as light to you. For you created my inmost being; you knit me together in my mother's womb. I praise you because I am fearfully and wonderfully made; your works are wonderful, I know that full well. My frame was not hidden from you when I was made in the secret place. When I was woven together in the depths of the earth, your eyes saw my unformed body. All the days ordained for me were written in your book before one of them came to be. How precious to me are your thoughts, O God! How vast is the sum of them! Were I to count them, they would outnumber the grains of sand. When I awake, I am still with you. Search me, O God, and know my heart; test me and know my anxious thoughts. See if there is any offensive way in me, and lead me in the way everlasting."

Psalm 139:1-18; 23-24

Doesn't this passage in Psalms just bless your heart? It reminds me of how special each of us are to our Creator and how much He cares about us in every way. God intimately loves me! God intimately loves you! Matthew 10:30 says: "And even the very hairs of your head are all numbered." This is amazing to me because I shed a lot of hair every day and God still knows how many strands of hair remain all the time. This conveys to us very clearly that God deeply cares about all the little details of our lives and He wants to be included in them.

If you can now begin to grasp how much God loves you, then you can go one step further and begin to understand how intricately He is working with each of us individually to help us to grow closer to Him. He knows us better than we know ourselves. Sometimes I pray that God would orchestrate circumstances in my life according to His sovereign understanding of who I really am. I am still growing in my understanding of myself and of whom I will continue to become, but He knows what I will become and how my thoughts will change. He can provide for my needs based on how I will be in the future. I have changed so much over the years that I have learned that often my prayers were prayed without a complete understanding of what I was asking for. God knows my heart now and He knows how my heart will be in the future. I can trust Him to take care of me in areas that I haven't yet gleaned a proper perspective or understanding of.

> *"God moves in a mysterious way,*
> *His wonders to perform;*
> *He plants His footsteps in the sea,*
> *And rides upon the storm.*
> *Deep in unfathomable mines*
> *Of never-failing skill,*
> *He treasures up His bright designs,*
> *And works His sovereign will."*
>
> *—William Cowper*

Springs in the Desert 10/3: "A Chinese man named Sai, had only one son and one horse. Once the horse ran away and Sai was very worried. Only one horse and lost! Someone said, "Don't suffer, wait a little." The horse came back. Not long after this the only son went out to the field riding the horse. Returning home he fell from the horse and broke his leg. What a sorrow had poor Sai then! He could not eat; he could not sleep; he could not even attend well to the wants of his son. Only one son and crippled! But someone said, "More patience, Sai!" Soon after the accident a war broke out. All the young men went to the war; none of them returned. Only Sai's son, the cripple, stayed at home, and remained to live long to his father's joy."

—Chinese Legend

God loves each one of us in such a special way. He knows how unique each of us are and what we struggle with through every step of our walk with Him. We can trust Him to not abandon us no matter how bleak our circumstances feel. He is in control; He is sovereign; and He is a loving and faithful Father.

> "For I know the plans I have for you," declares the Lord, "plans to prosper you and not to harm you, plans to give you hope and a future. Then you will call upon me and come and pray to me, and I will listen to you. You will seek me and find me when you seek me with all you heart. I will be found by you," declares the Lord.
>
> Jeremiah 29:11-14a

THANK YOU, LORD, FOR ALWAYS WALKING MY LIFE WITH ME!

ETERNITY DRIVES ME FORWARD

At the end of our earthly lives, God will judge all people according to who they lived for: themselves or God. Revelation 20:11-12 "Then I saw a great white throne and Him who was seated on it. Earth and sky fled from His presence, and there was no place for them. And I saw the dead, great and small, standing before the throne, and books were opened. Another book was opened, which is the book of life. The dead were judged according to what they had done as recorded in the books." His justice will prevail. People who reject God and His ways will be punished. The righteous who have obeyed God will be blessed and rewarded. When you are suffering, continue to be patient knowing that God's justice *will* come. Zephaniah 3:9 "Then will I purify the lips of the peoples, that all of them may call on the name of the Lord and serve Him shoulder to shoulder." Zephaniah 3:20 "At that time I will gather you; at that time I will bring you home. I will give you honor and praise among all the peoples of the earth when I restore your fortunes before your very eyes," says the Lord."

This topic was birthed in my heart after reading the book: *Driven by Eternity* by John Bevere. I suggest you read it. He helped me to view my life on this earth as temporary and my life in heaven as eternal. Our lives on this earth are just a speck of time compared to eternity. If we can really begin to grasp this difficult concept, then we will start to view our lives through very different eyes of perspective. We will begin to see our relationship with God and our impact on the lives of others as more important than just "getting ahead in life." They will become more of our focus rather than a stepping stone to a life goal.

John Bevere helped me grasp clearly that each of God's kids play a key role in His spiritual army and His plans *will* be fulfilled. Even if I fail to do my part, God will fill my spot with another willing and obedient servant-soldier.

Revelation 2:7 "He who has an ear, let him hear what the Spirit says to the churches. To him who overcomes, I will give the right to eat from the tree of life, which is in the paradise of God." John Bevere suggests that when we stand before God as believers, after our lives have been reviewed by Him, then we will eat of this tree of life and it will remove all of the "yuck" of this world and leave us clean again before God. Doesn't that sound beautiful?

Revelation 3:5 "He who overcomes will, like them; be dressed in white. I will never blot out his name from the book of life, but will acknowledge his name before my Father and His angels." John Bevere tells stories from people who have been to heaven and described how wonderful it is and how they wanted to stay there rather than come back to their earthly lives. His stories removed some of my fears of the unknown of heaven. He shared how people know and remember and greet one another when we arrive and how wonderful it is to be in the presence of God.

Revelation 2:23b "Then all the churches will know that I am He who searches hearts and minds, and I will repay each of you according to your deeds." He also shows how we will be rewarded in heaven for walking the narrow road toward maturity in Christ which is mostly what *Driven by Eternity* is about. We don't always see a reward for our Godly choices here on earth, but we will see them in heaven. This understanding was a huge encouragement to me to keep pressing on and to not ever give up.

> "Therefore we do not lose heart. Though outwardly we are wasting away, yet inwardly we are being renewed day by day. For our light and momentary troubles are achieving for us an eternal glory that far outweighs them all. So we fix our eyes not on what is seen, but on what is unseen. For what is seen is temporary, but what is unseen is eternal."
>
> 2 Peter 3:10-14

> "What He opens no one can shut, and what he shuts no one can open. I know your deeds. See, I have placed before you an open door that no one can shut. I know that you have little strength, yet you have kept my Word and have not denied my Name. I will make those who are of the synagogue of Satan,...fall down at your feet and acknowledge that I have loved you. Since you have kept my command to endure

patiently, I will also keep you from the hour of trial that is going to come upon the whole world to test those who live on the earth. I am coming soon. Hold on to what you have, so that no one will take your crown. Him who overcomes I will make a pillar in the temple of my God and the name of the city of my God, the new Jerusalem, which is coming down out of heaven from my God; and I will also write on him my new name. He who has an ear, let him hear what the Spirit says to the churches."

Revelation 3:7b-13

"But the day of the Lord will come like a thief. The heavens will disappear with a roar; the elements will be destroyed by fire, and the earth and everything in it will be laid bare. Since everything will be destroyed in this way, what kind of people ought you to be? You ought to live holy and godly lives as you look forward to the day of God and speed its coming. That day will bring about the destruction of the heavens by fire, and the elements will melt in the heat. But in keeping with his promise we are looking forward to a new heaven and a new earth, the home of righteousness. So then, dear friends, since you are looking forward to this, make every effort to be found spotless, blameless and at peace with him."

2 Peter 3:10-14

Don't be deceived into thinking that God is an indulgent heavenly grandfather, who is nice to have around, but really doesn't care about how we live our lives. God is holy and He will actively judge and justly punish everyone who is content to live in sin and is indifferent to Him. He will also reward His faithful and obedient servants. Be reminded that "the great day of the Lord's return *is near*."

WE NEED TO LIVE OUR LIVES…
DRIVEN BY ETERNITY!

FOCUS ON TODAY!

"BE STILL AND KNOW THAT I AM GOD!"

Psalm 46:10

"But he said to me, "My grace is sufficient for you, for my power is made perfect in weakness." Therefore I will boast all the more gladly about my weaknesses, so that Christ's power may rest on me."

2 Corinthians 12:9

My grace *is* sufficient for you! This is a present tense phrase. God wants us to focus on the now…on this moment in time. In the blink of an eye this moment will be forever gone into our past never to be used again. If we forget to focus on the *now*, we miss out on fond memories that will line our past as well as miss opportunities that will shape our future. This is an area I often struggle with when I'm with my family and I have a lot on my mind or my list of duties still needs to be done. I have to consciously remind myself to 'focus on my family' and not let my mind or my actions wander. If I don't work on this, my family will begin to feel less important than what I am focused on and that is not the message I want to convey. We all have to focus on enjoying each moment of the day that we are living…*when we are living it*. We miss out on so much because we are in a hurry or in a bad mood. Enjoy each moment because tomorrow is not a guarantee.

Satan loves to get us to focus on our past…all of our failures. This usually causes us to feel depressed (which is fear turned inward), discouraged, and victimized. Notice, that we just missed the *now* fretting about the past that we can't change. The truth is that if we have already asked forgiveness from Jesus for those past sins, then they are covered by His blood…they no longer exist. Don't allow Satan to take you down memory lane in this harmful way. God doesn't care about your past because He is masterful at re-shaping us from our past into fine vessels of use for His Kingdom purposes.

God says in Joel 2:25a: "And I will restore and replace for you the years the locusts have eaten." (Amplified) God saves everybody from the wrong path! He is the only one who can turn bad things into good. Instead, He wants your present and your future.

Satan will also try to get us to focus negatively on our future by filling us with thoughts of worry and fear about what tomorrow holds. 'Fear' is the enemy prophesying over us about a future *without God*. The way to overcome fear is to praise God. Tomorrow is something we cannot control by worrying about it anyway. Again, we lost out on the *now* by worrying about tomorrow. God holds our future in His hands. He knows each of our numbered days. He will provide for us just like He takes care of everything He has created.

> "Then Jesus said to his disciples: "Therefore I tell you, do not worry about your life, what you will eat; or about your body, what you will wear.

Coffee Talk

Life is more than food, and the body more than clothes. Consider the ravens: They do not sow or reap, they have no storeroom or barn; yet God feeds them. And how much more valuable you are than birds! *Who of you by worrying can add a single hour to his life?* Since you cannot do this very little thing, why do you worry about the rest? Consider how the lilies grow. They do not labor or spin. Yet I tell you, not even Solomon in all his splendor was dressed like one of these. If that is how God clothes the grass of the field, which is here today and tomorrow is thrown into the fire, how much more will he clothe you, O you of little faith! And do not set your heart on what you will eat or drink; do not worry about it. For the pagan world runs after all such things, and your Father knows that you need them. But seek his kingdom and these things will be given to you as well."

Luke 12:22-31

"I lift up my eyes to the hills—where does my help come from?

My help comes from the Lord, the Maker of heaven and earth.

He will not let your foot slip—he who watches over you will not slumber;

Indeed, he who watches over Israel will neither slumber nor sleep.

The Lord watches over you—the Lord is your shade at your right hand;

The sun will not harm you by day, nor the moon by night.

The Lord will keep you from all harm—he will watch over your life;

The Lord will watch over your coming and going both now and forevermore."

Psalm 121

Springs in the Desert: "*The other evening I found myself staggering alone under a load that was heavy enough to crush half a dozen strong men. After sheer exhaustion I put it down and had a good look at it. I found that it was all borrowed; part of it belonged to the following day; part of it belonged to the following week—and here was I borrowing it that it might crush me now! It is a very stupid, but a very ancient blunder.*"

—F.W. Boreham

AS YOU LEARN TO LIVE YOUR
LIFE IN THE NOW…
YOUR INNER MAN WILL BE STILL
AND REST IN YOUR GOD!

THE LAW OF OPPOSITION: GROW OR DIE

"He who has an ear, let him hear what the Spirit says to the churches. To him who overcomes, I will give the right to eat from the tree of life, which is in the paradise of God."

Revelation 2:7

In My Utmost for His Highest, *Oswald Chambers writes the following:*

"Life without war is impossible in the natural or the supernatural realm. It is a fact that there is a continuing struggle in the physical, mental, moral, and spiritual areas of life.

Health is the balance between the physical parts of my body and all the things and forces surrounding me.

Morally it is the same. Anything that does not strengthen me morally is the enemy of virtue within me. Whether I overcome, thereby producing virtue depends on the level of moral excellence in my life. But we must fight to be moral. Morality does not happen by accident; moral virtue is acquired.

And spiritually it is also the same. Jesus said, "In the world you will have tribulation…" (John 16:33). This means that anything which is not spiritual leads to my downfall. Jesus went on to say, "…but be of good cheer, I have overcome the world." I must learn to fight against and overcome the things that come against me, and in that way produce the balance of holiness. Then it becomes a delight to meet opposition.

Holiness is the balance between my nature and the law of God as expressed in Jesus Christ."

We are all under pressure from family, friends, jobs, school, clubs, church and more to perform our many life responsibilities. All of these things are good, but we have to be aware when they begin to steal all of our time and energy and leave us with nothing left to offer God. They can easily become the "better" that keeps us from the "best." Our values and priorities are reflected in how we spend our time, money, and talents. We say that God is our number one priority, but do our actions prove our words? This trap is one of Satan's best tactics with believers. In the book of Haggai, the Israelites stopped rebuilding the temple and only focused on beautifying their own homes. However, the harder they worked to "get ahead," the less they had because their spiritual growth was no longer a priority. The same happens to us. If we put God first, He will provide for all our deepest needs. If we have Him in any other order, our lives will begin to crumble. God withholds His blessing when He no longer has first place in our lives because He is a God who is jealous for a personal relationship with us. Hebrews 5:14 "But solid food is for the mature, who by constant use have trained themselves to distinguish good from evil."

We are either moving forward in our relationship with God or drifting further away from Him. Women of God, whatever we do we must keep growing in our relationship with God! We must keep allowing Him to shape and mold us into His image. Everything we've talked about in this book offers us avenues and areas of growth that can lead us closer to Him. The law of opposition says that if we are not growing, then we are dying. There is no such thing as "status quo" in our spiritual walks. None of us want to go backwards in our spiritual lives. But if we are not applying ourselves to growth in Christ, we will begin to drift away from Him and start to die. Even if we are standing still, it will lead us down the road to death because to stand still means that we are stagnant. Haggai 2:10-14 is an example of the following truths. *Holiness will not rub off on others, but the sinful influence of others can easily contaminate us.* This is such a well-traveled path by many believers. We all know Christians who were once passionate for God and are now distant from Him. Don't be deceived by this common deception of the enemy. Don't be left behind in your relationship with God.

> "But you, (wo)man of God, flee from all this, and pursue righteousness, godliness, faith, love, endurance and gentleness. Fight the good fight of faith. Take hold of the eternal life to which you were called when you made your good confession in the presence of many witnesses." (emphasis added)
>
> I Timothy 6:11-12

The return of Jesus at an unknown time is not a trap or a trick to catch us off guard. In fact, God is delaying the return of His Son in order to bring more people to a saving knowledge of Him. He wants to populate heaven with his creation: people. God desires to use His children here on earth to touch many more lives with a living, vibrant relationship with their Creator. Luke 12:35-40 "Be dressed and ready for service and keep your lamps burning, like men waiting for their master to return from a wedding banquet, so that when he comes and knocks they can immediately open the door for him. It will be good for those servants whose master finds them watching when he comes. I tell you the truth, he will dress himself to serve, will have them recline at the table and will come and wait on them. It will be good for those servants whose master finds them ready, even if he comes in the second or third watch of the night. But understand this: If the owner of the house had known at what hour the thief was coming, he would not have let his house be broken into. You also must be ready, because the Son of Man will come at an hour when you do not expect him."

We have to be ready for the return of Jesus by obeying "His Word." John 1:1-5 says: "In the beginning was the Word, and the Word was with God, and *the Word was God*." He was with God in the beginning. Through him all things were made; without him nothing was made that has been made. In him was life, and that life was the light of men. The light shines in the darkness, but the darkness has not understood it." Only the Word of God through the power of the Holy Spirit can lead us into truth and help us to conform to God's ways. Hebrews 4:12-13 "For the word of God is living and active. Sharper than any double-edged sword, it penetrates even to dividing soul and spirit, joints and marrow; it judges the thoughts and attitudes of the heart. Nothing in all creation is hidden from God's sight. Everything is uncovered and laid bare before the eyes of him to whom we must give account." The Bible is a gift from God that He uses to communicate His ideas. It is living and life-changing. With precision, God's Word reveals who we are deep down inside as well as whom we are not. It penetrates to the center of who we are in our soul: mind, will, and emotions and reveals the good and evil within. Finally, it demands a response to either obey or reject its truths. Keep in mind that nothing about you can be hidden from God. He knows all our secrets, even the ones we are hiding from. But in spite of our sin, He still loves us and wants to develop an intimate relationship with us built on love and trust.

Haggai 2:6-9 "This is what the Lord Almighty says: 'In a little while I will once more shake the heavens and the earth, the sea and the dry land. I will shake all nations, and the desired of all nations will come, and I will fill this house with glory,' says the Lord Almighty. 'The silver is mine and the gold is mine,' declares the Lord Almighty. 'The glory of this present house will be greater than the glory of the former house,' says the Lord Almighty. 'And in this place I will grant peace,' declares the Lord Almighty." God doesn't need us, but because of His love for us He chooses to use us to partner with Him to fulfill His eternal Kingdom plans. He will provide everything that we need, but we must be willing to be His vessels of use. Are you available for God to use to reach a lost and dying world with

His love? God often sends His encouragement and approval after we take our first few steps of obedience. God is eager to bless us! God is pleased when we give Him first place in our lives. He promises to give us His strength and guidance when we do. Whenever you get discouraged, remind yourself, "God has chosen me!"

I pray that "my road" and the lessons I have learned along the way are an encouragement to you on "your road." He is teaching us all the same things in different ways and at different times.

> PRESS IN TO GOD, THE GREAT "I AM,"
> WHO IS THE AUTHOR AND
> FINISHER OF OUR FAITH!
> HE IS MAKING US INTO HIS PURE
> AND SPOTLESS BRIDE!

> "BE ON YOUR GUARD. STAND FIRM IN THE FAITH; BE (WO)MEN OF COURAGE; BE STRONG. DO EVERYTHING IN LOVE!" (emphasis added)
>
> I Corinthians 16:13-14

SICKNESS

Time for Everything

There is a time for everything, and a season for every activity under the heavens: a time to be born and a time to die, a time to plant and a time to uproot, a time to kill and a time to heal, a time to tear down and a time to build, a time to weep and a time to laugh, a time to mourn and a time to dance, a time to scatter stones and a time to gather them, a time to embrace and a time to refrain from embracing, a time to search and a time to give up, a time to keep and a time to throw away, a time to tear and a time to mend, a time to be silent and a time to speak, a time to love and a time to hate, a time for war and a time for peace. What do workers gain from their toil? I have seen the burden God has laid on the human race. He has made everything beautiful in its time. He has also set eternity in the human heart; yet no one can fathom what God has done from beginning to end.

Ecclesiastes 3:1-10

How do you look at life? Do you subconsciously think things will always be how they currently are...whether it is good or bad? Life is not that way! Every aspect of life is full of many various seasons and we need to acknowledge those seasons in order to prepare our hearts to navigate life more smoothly when the seasons do change. If we are completely honest with ourselves, as much as we say we don't like change, we all get bored without it. Change is the essence of living! Bob Hamp says: "Familiarity with people, routines, relationships and religious systems can numb us all to sleep! *The struggles of life act as a wake-up-call sometimes.*" (Think Differently; Live Differently)

When you are walking a difficult set of circumstances in life, don't believe the lie that things will always be this difficult and never change. It is impossible because life is ever-changing. Likewise, when life is rich and full of the desires of our hearts, we must trust God in whatever circumstance He allows to darken that season. Please know His end goal is to bring character and depth into our lives as we allow God to walk us through it step by step. James 1:2-5 "Consider it pure joy, my brothers and sisters, whenever you face trials of many kinds, because you know that the testing of your faith produces perseverance. Let perseverance finish its work so that you may be mature and complete, not lacking anything. If any of you lacks wisdom, you should ask God, who gives generously to all without finding fault, and it will be given to you."

Serious health issues eventually come into all of our lives, either to us personally or to a loved one because we are in a fallen world. We all view sickness as a game of Russian roulette, hoping we are not the next victim. Some of us live in denial of it due to our youth or we try to take care of ourselves through health remedies to avoid it, but ultimately we all walk through life not knowing when our turn will be.

When our four children were little and we were so dependant on Gary to provide for us and keep all the bills paid, I remember praying and asking God to not allow serious sickness to impact our lives while the children were young. I just didn't feel like I could handle it. I Corinthians 10:13 says: "No temptation has overtaken you except what is common to mankind. And God is faithful; he will not let you be tempted beyond what you can bear. But when you are tempted, he will also provide a way out so that you can endure it." God honored this prayer. Once our children were all older my husband Gary began the road of serious sickness in 2010. He threw up daily for a year with the doctors diagnosing him with pneumonia three times. The day after Christmas 2011 the doctor called me and said Gary's blood work had serious signs of major health issues and I needed to take him to the emergency room immediately. We did not have health insurance so this phone call was scary on two levels: health and finances. I told Gary who said he would not go because we couldn't afford it. I turned to God in prayer and asked what to do? As I prayed I felt the Lord say for me not to worry, and that He would provide. He told me to take Gary to the emergency room. I sought council from my nurse neighbor as to what hospital to go to that was more affordable and that is where we went. They admitted him and he was there from December 26th-January 2nd. He was diagnosed with the beginning stages of kidney failure and they removed 30 pounds of water weight from his body over 3 days. He was also diagnosed with type 2 diabetes that lasted a year which I believe was due to throwing up the previous year which caused a chemical imbalance in his body. He no longer requires medicine for diabetes…glory to God. Gary came home weak and our family worked as a team to help him with his food and exercise routine in addition to running the day care to maintain our family income. Due to our low income the previous year, the hospital secured financial aid to pay the $40,000.00 hospital bill. GLORY TO GOD! The Lord helped us pay the doctor bills as well. When you do not have insurance the doctors will give a discount to help the bill to be paid.

Then in March 2012, Gary said he no longer had peripheral vision in his right eye and he was scared. We mentioned it to a nurse friend and she said to go to the ER again. Once there they ran a CAT scan on Gary and admitted him again for another week. He had to have an MRI which showed what they expected. He had had three mini-strokes. He has always struggled with claustrophobia and it took a sedative to get him into the MRI machine after he unsuccessfully begged me many times to not make him take the test. The strokes had left him with a temporary child-like mentality. They needed to know if the strokes were caused by his heart or blood pressure to know how to correctly treat him to prevent more strokes. Gary was released on my 42nd birthday, March 23. He came home as a little child, dependant on us all. He repetitively thanked each of us every few minutes for taking such good care of him, forgetting he had just said thank you. He lost the privilege of driving, cooking, or using knives in the kitchen. He struggled walking as his depth perception was off. He needed help showering and shaving and basic living skills. God met our family with the strength each of us needed to care for Gary's needs and allow him the time he needed to grow and heal. I had to step into the role as the head of our home for the first time in my life. And God was my ever present help in time of need. God gave me a special strength and courage to face the current challenges and not lose hope. This time God paid off the $42,000.00 hospital stay leaving us with a balance of $5,000.00 that I still make monthly payments to. God again helped us pay off the doctor bills as well. The Lord had loved ones send us money and each time a new doctor bill came I had enough to pay them. His grace and provision during that season was so incredible! God also had one of our close friends, Stacey Cole, come faithfully and tutor Gary's mind with games to help him heal from the stroke and help him to be able to read clearly again. We are so thankful for her servant heart toward our family. Due to Gary's health issues we had to step out from being pastors to take care of him and our family. Gary did earn back the privileges of driving, using knives and cooking within about six months.

Most of 2013 Gary struggled with mental loss from the kidney failure. Kidney failure affects our brains due to the toxin levels in our blood that are not filtered out. I remember having a conversation with the Lord around the 15 year mark in our marriage. I told the Lord that

He had blessed me so richly with Gary as a husband and our children and that if anything happened I would be thankful for the time I had already enjoyed. I realized that many people never get to experience what I had been blessed with for even a short time. I acknowledged then and there that I would have no room to complain if that season ended. The Lord reminded me of that conversation as I have walked the past year. Gary does not remember how we used to be…how we could read each other's minds or finish each other's thoughts. He doesn't remember many of the things I have shared in this book. Of course this is heart-breaking. He says he lives under a cloud that occasionally lifts. He became another person; only a shell of the man I once called husband. Communication has always been strong in our marriage, but kidney failure has turned him into someone where communication has been near impossible. I have walked the stages of grief from:

1. Shock/Denial
2. Pain/Guilt
3. Anger/Resentment/Hate
4. Depression/ Reflection/Loneliness
5. The Upward Turn
6. Reconstruction and working through
7. Acceptance/Hope

I have walked this road with the Lord in my heart and quiet time with Him and He has loved me through every step of the process. My journal bears all the ugly emotions and depths of pain in my heart. God has been my faithful companion each and every step of the way. Through it all, God has become my husband at a whole new level. He is my strength…my confidant…my completer. God wants to be that to each one of us and the circumstances that life throws at us are the tools He uses in the process of teaching us how to allow Him to be all He wants to be in each of our lives.

> "For your Maker is your husband—
> the Lord Almighty is his name—
> the Holy One of Israel is your Redeemer;
> he is called the God of all the earth."
>
> Isaiah 54:5

October 21, 2013 Gary had surgery to create the ports for dialysis to begin in his body. After 4 dialysis treatments, my husband came back to me. I can't tell you how full my heart is with love for him and thankful to God for giving him back to me. I have missed him so much! Through it all God has been faithful and will continue to be as we continue to walk this road of the unknown future…with a known God.

CONCLUSION

THE PLAN OF SALVATION; REDEDICATION TO GOD

If you have never begun this relationship with God, I want to give you the opportunity to make that decision. God is made up of a triune headship: God the Father; God the Son; and God the Holy Spirit. They are all one God with three different roles that they play. A way to explain this is I am a woman who has three roles. I am a daughter, wife, and mother. I perform all three roles, yet in all three roles, I am still me. This is how I describe the Trinity.

God the Father, sent His one and only Son to earth as a human yet he was still fully God. The Holy Spirit planted the seed of Jesus in the womb of the virgin, Mary. She conceived and gave birth to Jesus and she and Joseph raised him. When Jesus was thirty years old he began his three-year earthly ministry. He healed the sick, performed creative miracles like growing out limbs and restoring eyesight, fed multitudes of people with small amounts of food, raised the dead back to life, and spoke incredible truths from the Father-heart of God. Then as was pre-planned by God, Jesus was betrayed, beaten, mocked, and crucified on a cross to die as the final substitute for all of our sins: past, present, and future. During those three days, Jesus went down to Hades and conquered death once and for all. After the three days, Jesus rose from the dead. He spent many days with His disciples teaching and encouraging them. Then they watched Him ascend into heaven. He left us with the command to go and make disciples of all nations. He also gave us the promise that He would be preparing heaven for us along with the promise to return for us and take us to be there with Him. After Jesus' resurrection God sent the promised Holy Spirit to comfort us and lead us into all truth. The Holy Spirit wants to walk with you every step of the way as you embark on this new relationship with God. This is what the Bible teaches about how to have an intimate and personal relationship with your Creator.

The first verse to understand the free gift of salvation is Romans 3:23, "For all have sinned, and come short of the glory of God." We have all sinned. We have all done things that are displeasing to God. There is no one who is innocent. Romans 3:10-12 " As it is written: There is no one righteous, not even one; there is no one who understands, no one who seeks God. All have turned away, they have together become worthless; there is no one who does good, not even one." This verse gives a detailed picture of what sin looks like in our lives.

The second Scripture to understand salvation teaches us about the consequences of sin. Romans 6:23 "For the wages of sin is death; but the gift of God is eternal life through Jesus Christ our Lord." The punishment that we have earned for our sins is death. Not just physical death, but eternal death!

The third verse on the road to understanding salvation declares "But God demonstrates His own love toward us, in that while we were still sinners, Christ died for us." Romans 5:8 Jesus Christ died for us individually! Jesus' death paid for the price of all of our sins. Jesus' resurrection proves that God accepted Jesus' death as the payment for our sins.

The fourth stop on the road to salvation is Romans 10:9, "that if you confess with your mouth Jesus as Lord, and believe in your heart that God raised Him from the dead, you will be saved." Because of Jesus' death on our behalf, all we have to do is believe in Him, trusting His death as the payment for our sins – and we will be saved! Romans 10:13 says it again, "for everyone who calls on the name of the Lord will be saved." Jesus died to pay the penalty for our sins and rescue us from eternal death. Salvation (the forgiveness of sins) is available to anyone who will trust in Jesus Christ as their Lord and Savior.

The final aspect to understand is the results of salvation. Romans 5:1 has this wonderful message, "Therefore, since we have been justified through faith, we have peace with God through our Lord Jesus Christ." Through Jesus Christ we can have a relationship of peace with God. Romans 8:1 teaches us, "Therefore, there is now no condemnation for those who are in Christ Jesus." Because of Jesus' death on our behalf, we will never be condemned for our sins. Finally, we have this precious promise of God from Romans 8:38-39, "For I am convinced that neither death nor life, neither angels nor demons, neither the present nor the future, nor any powers, neither height nor depth, nor anything else in all creation, will be able to separate us from the love of God that is in Christ Jesus our Lord."

The following Scriptures come from the book of Romans and are often referred to as the "Romans Road." Would you like to follow the Romans road to salvation? If so, here is a simple prayer you can pray to God. Saying a prayer is a way to declare to God that you are relying on Jesus Christ for your salvation. The words themselves will not save you. Only faith in Jesus Christ can provide salvation! *"God, I know that I have sinned against you and am deserving of punishment. But Jesus Christ took the punishment that I deserve so that through faith in Him I can be forgiven. With your help, I place my trust in Jesus for salvation. Thank you for your wonderful grace and forgiveness —and the gift of eternal life! Amen!"* {Now you need to get involved in a local, Christian, Bible-based church and be baptized in water to outwardly show your inner commitment to God.}

If you have already asked Jesus to be your Savior, but you have backslidden; God still wants you back! Would you like to re-dedicate your life to loving and serving Him with all your heart, soul, mind, and strength? If so, then pray the following prayer: *"God, I have walked away from You partly through disobedient choices I made and partly by becoming stagnant and no longer growing in my relationship with You. Will You please forgive me? I love You and want to come back home to You. Thank you for Your love and forgiveness and grace. Help me, Holy Spirit, as I begin again to develop my relationship with*

God. In Jesus' Name, Amen!" (Reference used: www.gotquestions.org)

I'M SO PROUD OF YOU! I'LL SEE YOU
IN HEAVEN IF I DON'T GET THE
PRIVILEDGE OF MEETING YOU
HERE ON EARTH!